中华五福
Designs of Chinese Blessings

Happiness

主 编/黄全信

副主编/黄迎 李进

编 委/吴曼丽 任晋英 陈铮 魏毅 金苋

贾小凯 戴斌 靳艺兵

翻 译/李迎春

华语教学出版社
SINOLINGUA

First Edition   2003

ISBN 7-80052-892-8

Copyright 2003 by Sinolingua

Published by Sinolingua

24 Baiwanzhuang Road, Beijing 100037, China

Tel: (86) 10-68995871/68326333

Fax: (86) 10-68326333

E-mail: hyjx @263.net

Printed by Beijing Foreign Languages Printing House

Distributed by China International

Book Trading Corporation

35 Chegongzhuang Xilu, P.O.Box 399

Beijing 100044, China

Printed in the People's Republic of China

目 录
contents

人臻五福　花满三春

　　吉祥一词，始见于《易经》："吉事有祥。"《左传》有："是何祥也？吉祥焉在？"《庄子》则有："虚室生日，吉祥止止。"《注疏》云："吉者，福善之事；祥者，嘉庆之征。"

　　吉祥二字，在甲骨文中被写作"吉羊"。上古人过着游牧生活，羊肥大成群是很"吉祥"的事，在古器物的铭文中多有"吉羊"。《说文》云："羊，祥也。"

　　吉祥，是美好、幸运的形象；吉祥，是人类最迷人的主题。艺术，最终都是把理想形象化；吉祥图，是中华吉祥文化最璀璨的明珠。旧时有联："善果皆欢喜，香云普吉祥。"吉祥图有：吉祥如意、五福吉祥等。

　　五福，是吉祥的具体。福、禄、寿、喜、财，在民间被称为五福；福星、禄星、寿星、喜神、财神，在仙界被尊为五福神。五福最早见于《尚书》："五福：一曰寿，二曰富，三曰

康宁，四曰攸好德，五曰考终命。"旧时有联："三阳临吉地，五福萃华门。"吉祥图有：五福捧寿、三多五福等。

福，意为幸福美满。《老子》："福兮，祸所伏。"《韩非子》："全富贵之谓福。"旧时有联："香焚一炷，福赐三多。"吉祥图有：福在眼前、纳福迎祥、翘盼福音、天官赐福等。

禄，意为高官厚禄。《左传》："介之推不言禄，禄亦弗及。"《汉书》："身宠而载高位，家温而食厚禄。"旧时有联："同科十进士，庆榜三名元。"吉祥图有：禄位高升、福禄寿禧、天赐禄爵、加官进禄等。

寿，意为健康长寿。《庄子》："人，上寿百岁，中寿八十，下寿六十。"《诗经》："如南山之寿，不骞不崩。"旧时有联："同臻寿域，共跻春台。"吉祥图有：寿星高照、鹤寿千年、富贵寿考、蟠桃献寿等。

喜，意为欢乐喜庆。《国语》："固庆其喜而吊其忧。"韦昭注："喜犹福也。"旧时有联："笑到几时方合口，坐来无日不开怀。"吉祥图有：喜上眉梢、双喜临门、端阳喜庆、皆大欢喜等。

财，意为发财富有。《荀子》："务本节用财无极。"旧时有联："生意兴隆通四海，财源茂盛达三江。"吉祥图有：财源滚滚、招财进宝、喜交财运、升官发财等。

吉祥图，不仅有"五福"之内涵，而且是

绘画艺术和语言艺术的珠联璧合。在绘画上，体现了中国画主要的表现手段——线的魅力，给人以美感，令人赏心悦目。吉祥图虽多出自民间画工之手，却多有顾恺之"春蚕吐丝"之韵，曹仲达"曹衣出水"之美，吴道子"吴带当风"之妙；在语言上，通俗和普及了古代文化，吉祥图多配有一句浓缩成四个字的吉语祥词，给人以吉祥，令人心驰神往。

《中华五福吉祥图典》，汇集了我数代家传和几十年收藏的精品吉祥图，可谓美不胜收。其中既有明之典雅，又有清之华丽；既有皇家之富贵，又有民间之纯朴；既有北方之粗犷，又有南方之秀美……按五福全书分成福、禄、寿、喜、财五集，每集吉祥图 119 幅，共 595 幅。除同类图案外，均按笔画顺序编排。基本包括了中国传统吉祥图的各个方面，并对每幅图作了考证和诠释，使之图文并茂，相得益彰。

五福人人喜，吉祥家家乐。吉祥图是中国的，也是世界的，故以汉英对照出版。《中华五福吉祥图典》会给您带来吉祥，给您全家带来幸福。

黄全信于佩实斋
2003 年 1 月 1 日

中华五福吉祥图典

喜

福 禄 寿 喜 财

May People Enjoy a Life Full of Blessings, and Let Flowers Bloom Throughout Spring Time

The word jixiang (meaning lucky, propitious, or auspicious) is mentioned in Chinese ancient books and writings as early as in the Zhou Dynasty.

The word jixiang was written as jiyang (lucky sheep) on oracle bones. To the ancient Chinese, who led a nomadic life, large herds of well-fed sheep were auspicious things, and the word jiyang also appeared in engravings on ancient utensils.

To have good luck is mankind's eternal desire. While art records man's ideals, good luck pictures are the most brilliant part of the Chinese good luck culture. An old couplet says that kindness leads to happiness and good luck. Typical good luck pictures are: good luck and heart's content, good luck with five blessings, etc.

The five blessings – good fortune, high salary and a good career, longevity, happiness, and wealth – are the concrete forms of good luck , and there are five kinds of gods presiding over these blessings. The five blessings as they are first mentioned in Chinese literature are not quite the same as the five which are talked about today, though they are quite similar. An old couplet says that as the land of good luck bathes in the Sun, a prosperous family is granted all the blessings. Typical good luck pictures are: long-term enjoyment of all five blessings, more blessings, etc.

Good fortune means happiness and complete satisfaction. Ancient Chinese philosophers, including Lao Zi, all commented on the notion of good fortune. An old couplet says to burn incense to beg for more blessings. Good luck pictures in this theme include good fortune for today, blessings from above, etc.

High salary means handsome salaries at prestigious posts. In old times, Chinese attached great significance to academic excellence, which led in turn to high positions in government. An old couplet says may you distinguish yourselves in the royal examinations and rank at the top of the list. Good luck pictures in this theme used in this book include big improvements in salary and post, salary and position bestowed from heaven, etc.

Longevity refers to good health and a long life. As Zhuangzhou said, and the *Book of Songs* records, longevity is the universal wish of mankind. As wished in an old couplet, to grow to a long life together is a joyful experience. This book has the following good luck pic -

tures concerning longevity: high above shines the star of longevity, live to be 1, 000 years with white hair, and offer the flat peach to wish for longevity, etc.

Happiness refers to happy events and celebrations. Happy events should be celebrated, while those with worries should be consoled according to ancient Chinese literature. An old Chinese couplet says, why not keep on laughing as all days are filled with happiness. Good luck pictures on this theme included in this book include double happiness visits at the door, all's well that ends well, etc.

Wealth means getting rich and having plentiful things. Ancient Chinese believed that the secret to endless wealth is to be down-to-earth and prudent. Illustrating the concept of wealth is an old couplet: a prosperous business deals with people from all corners of the world, and wealth rolls in from afar. Typical good luck pictures of this type include in comes wealth, get rich and win high positions, etc.

Good luck pictures not only incorporate the five blessings but the art of painting and language as well. The beautiful lines of these pictures, done in the style of traditional Chinese painting, provide the viewers with artistic enjoyment which is pleasing to the eyes and heart. Though mostly the work of folk artists, they exhibit a level of craftsmanship worthy of the great and famous masters. The language adopted in these pictures

Designs of Chinese Blessings

serves to popularize ancient culture, and the four-character good luck phrase accompanying almost every picture depicts an attractive scene.

Designs of Chinese Blessings is a compilation of special good luck pictures passed down in my family forseveral generations as well those which I have been collecting for dozens of years. Their beauty is beyond description. They combine the elegance of the Ming Dynasty and the magnificence of the Qing Dynasty, the nobility of the royal family and the modesty of the common people, the boldness of the north and the delicacy of the south. The book consists of five sections: good fortune, high salary and a good career, longevity, happiness, and wealth. With 119 pictures in each section, the whole book contains 595 pictures and is a complete representation of the various aspects of traditional Chinese good luck pictures. On top of this, research has been done on each picture, and the interpretations complement the visuals nicely.

As the five blessings are the aspiration of each individual, good luck delights all households. The good luck pictures originated in China and their good message should benefit all people of this world. May the *Designs of Chinese Blessings* bring good luck to your life and happiness to your family.

Huang Quanxin
Jan.1, 2003

一团和气

Intimacy with He (Shen)

"一团和气图"初创于明"酒狂仙客",画一道士盘坐一团,谓儒、道、释原为一气而成。《锄经书舍零墨》:和珅曾为吴白华侍郎之弟子,后和珅登相位,吴反拜和门下。和败被刑,有人赠吴一团和气图,讽吴有一团和珅之气。

The picture was created by a Ming Dynasty scholar. The picture features a Taoist priest sitting all rounded up, indicating that Confucianism, Taoism, and Buddhism came from common roots. Record has it that He Shen, the notorious rotten official of the Qing Dynasty was once a student of another official Wu and when He Shen became Prime Minister, Wu became a follower of He. Upon He's collapse and sentence, this picture was given to Wu as a gift to ridicule Wu who was close to He Shen.

◎中华五福吉祥图典

喜

福 禄 寿 喜 财

一团和气

Harmony and kindness

阿福是我国南方民间流行的泥塑，手执"和气吉祥"之横联。旧时正月初九是玉皇诞辰，玉帝又名天公，是道教的首神。初九要祭天公，此日讲究和气，不能冒犯天神。旧时非常讲究和气，做买卖和气生财，在家和和睦睦。

This picture features "Afu", a clay statue popular in south China with a horizontal couplet in the hands that reads "kindness leads to happiness". In the past, the ninth day of the first month of the lunar year is regarded as the birthday of the Heavenly God, the head of Taoism. Rituals are to be performed and sacrifices offered to him on that day. Kindness is the focus on that day and no offense shall be made. Harmony was highly treasured in the past both for business and families.

中华五福吉祥图典

喜

福禄寿喜财

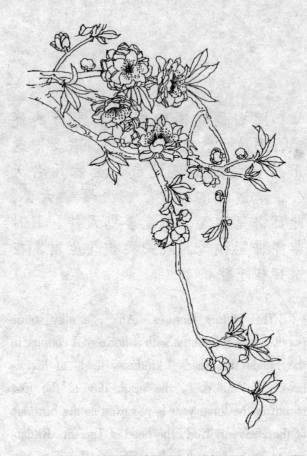

九重春色

Long-lasting beauty
of spring

唐·杜甫诗："五夜漏声催晓箭，九重春色醉仙桃。"九，数之极也，泛指多。九重，多层也，指天或宫禁。碧桃花，是桃的变种。春季开花，色粉红至深红，盛开时花红似火，春意盎然。"九重春色"寓意美好春光长留人间。

The idiom originates from a poem by Du Fu of the Tang Dynasty. In the poem, he described the beauty of the spring season by focusing on the profoundly intoxicating scent of peach blossoms that are either pink, scarlet, or even fiery, displaying the unique liveliness of spring to its fullness. The picture implies a wish for the long-lasting beauty of spring on earth.

◎中华五福吉祥图典

喜

福 禄 寿 喜 财

子孙万代

Thousands of generations
of offsprings

福禄

　　葫芦原产印度，传入我国后各地多有栽培。因其形状奇特，成熟后色泽金黄，在我国传统文化中往往带有神秘色彩。"葫芦"与"福禄"谐音，更为人所喜。葫芦为男女合体，且多子，示"子孙"。"蔓带"谐"万代"。寓意子孙万代吉祥。

Gourd, now planted all over China, first came from India. Their peculiar shape and golden color when mature imply a sense of mystery in traditional Chinese culture. People like gourds because they sound similar to "blessings and fortune" in Chinese. As gourds are androgynous and bear a lot of seeds, they are associated with offsprings. The picture implies peace and happiness to thousands of generations of offsprings.

中华五福吉祥图典

喜

福 禄 寿 喜 财

子孙万代

Thousands of generations
of offsprings

石榴多子，葫芦爬蔓，在吉祥图中都是"多子"的象征。葫芦为男女合体并多子，喻"子孙"葫芦有"蔓带"，与"万代"谐音，合为"子孙万代"。图中两位可爱的童子，在玩赏有蔓带的葫芦，来表示"子孙万代"家族兴旺之福。

Pomegranates bear a lot of seeds and bottle gourds have vines. They are both symbols of a large number of offsprings in images of happiness. The androgynous and seed-bearing bottle gourds with vines indicate thousands of generations of off-springs. In the picture, two lovely kids are play-ing with bottle gourds on the vine, a sign of family prosperity.

万代常春

*Youth and vitality for
all generations of people*

闻一多《伏羲考》："汉族以葫芦为伏羲女娲本身。"葫芦的谐音为"护禄"、"福禄"。蔓为带状植物茎，"蔓带"与"万代"谐音。月季花又称为长春花，四时艳丽，被誉为"花中皇后"，称为"天下风流"。祝愿世世代代永葆青春。

"Bottle gourds" sound similar to "happiness and fortune" in Chinese while "vines on a plant" reads like "thousands of generations of offsprings" in Chinese pronunciation. Chinese roses or ever-green roses bloom all year round and have won such titles as queen of flowers. The picture wishes youth and vitality to all generations of people.

中华五福吉祥图典

喜

福 禄 寿 喜 财

万事大吉

Fine and complete

in everything

　　瓷瓶颈围上的"卐"字，与瓶中的柿子，谐音合为"万事"。又瓶旁的百合，与瓶中的柿子，谐音合为"百事"。大桔子谐音喻大吉。为万事大吉，或百事大吉。旧时也有"万事大吉"演绎出的"万事大结"，即所有的事都办了。

In the picture，the symbol 卐 on the bottle neck and the persimmons in the bottle as well as the lilies next to the bottle can be read to mean "all things". The large oranges mean good fortune. So this picture means everything is fine or everything is complete.

◎中华五福吉祥图典

喜

福 禄 寿 喜 财

万事如意

Smooth and heart-contented

in all things

民间视万年青为吉祥物，一者其名吉祥，二者为多年生常绿草本植物。"柿"谐音"事"，合为"万事"。灵芝是神奇应瑞之草，《瑞应图》："芝英者，王者德仁则生。"如意的顶端多做成灵芝形，故在吉祥图中多以灵芝喻如意。

Chinese folk customs regard rohdea japonica as an object of happiness because of the lucky name it bears and also due to the fact that it is an ever-green plant. This green plant and persimmons together sound the same as "all things" in Chinese. The glossy ganoderma is a fungus associated with magic and luck. As the head of a *ruyi* (a traditional Chinese display object of happiness and fortune) is often crafted into the shape of a glossy ganoderma, the fungus has itself evolved to mean happiness and fortune in images of this type.

◎中华五福吉祥图典

喜

福禄寿喜财

马上平安

Peace on horse back

《名臣言行录》："胡安定读书泰山，十年不归，得家书，见平安二字，即投涧中，不复展读。"又唐诗："马上相逢无纸笔，凭君传语报平安。"古代交通不便，多靠骑马驰送家书，故家书难得。马上平安是对平安的祝愿。

Old Chinese literature records that a scholar that had gone far afield to engage in studies and who had remained absent for 10 years would decline going on reading a letter from home as soon as he found the character "peace" on it. Poetry also relates that messages of peace and safety should be sent home verbally as paper and pen were not handy when carried on horsebacks. Letters from home were hard to come by in the past as traffic solely consisted of horses. The picture is a wish for peace and safety.

中华五福吉祥图典

喜 福 禄 寿 喜 财

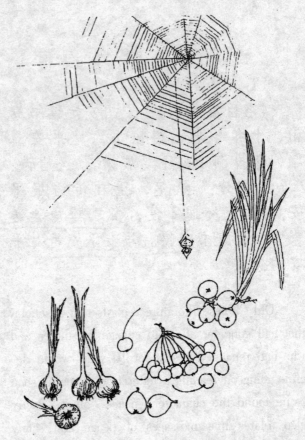

天中集瑞

All good fortune gathered

菖蒲

　　"天中集瑞"是旧时端午节人们祝颂吉祥的图饰。《熙朝乐事》："端午为天中节。"图中集五种祥瑞之物。菖蒲，叶可编织端午节令的各种用具。樱桃，寓福寿延年。枇杷，备四时之气。蒜，可祛除五毒。蜘蛛又称喜蛛，寓意喜从天降。

The picture came from celebrations for the Dragon Boat Festival in the past and indicates happiness and fortune. The Dragon Boat Festival is actually the mid junction of the lunar year. The five items in the image, calamus, cherry, loquat, garlic, and spider, are all objets of happiness and fortune. The spider, nicknamed lucky spider, here conveys the meaning of a heaven-sent fortune.

◎中华五福吉祥图典

喜

福禄寿喜财

喜 *Happiness*

天从人愿

*May heaven follow
the will of man*

《荀子·天论》："天行有常，不为尧存，不为桀亡。应之以治则吉，应之以乱则凶。"自古认为天是永恒的，天意不可违。但人们多么祈盼老天能顺应人的心愿。图中天竹取其"天"，灵芝中有人字取其"人"，合为"天从人愿"。

As ancient Chinese literature has it, there are eternal rules in the universe that shall not be violated. Yet strong and persistent are the wishes of people cherishing that the universal rules be consistent with the will of man. The picture here carries the meaning of "heaven" and "man" from the two plants drawn here and combines to convey the wish that heaven follow the will of man.

中华五福吉祥图典

喜

福 禄 寿 喜 财

天仙送子

New-born babies sent
by the fairies

家中生个宝贝儿子，是中国传统观念中的头等大事。《孟子·离娄上》："不孝有三，无后为大。"《春秋公羊传·隐公元年》："母以子为贵。"在明、清以至民国时期，有关"送子"题材的吉祥风俗年画处处可见。

In traditional Chinese concepts, a son born to the household is of paramount significance, one who fails to bring offspring to one's clan is regarded as a shameful figure, and a woman with children is deemed a respectful member of the family. During the Ming and Qing dynasties as well as the rule of the Republic of China, Chinese New Year pictures featuring new-born babies sent by the fairies are extremely popular.

◎中华五福吉祥图典

喜

福 禄 寿 喜 财

双喜同心

Devoted newlyweds

作为吉祥物，鸳鸯是纯真爱情、美满婚姻的象征，在汉代就有了以鸳鸯为题材的吉祥图。在喜庆婚联中常有："鸳鸯比翼，夫妻同心。"，"缕结同心日丽屏间孔雀，莲开并蒂影瑶池上鸳鸯"等。吉祥图"双喜同心"多用于婚庆。

As the symbol of pure love and happy marriage, mandarin ducks have appeared on pictures featuring happiness and fortune since the Han Dynasty. In couplets that celebrate and praise the loyalty and ties of new couples, mandarin ducks serve as the embodiment of human love. The picture is frequently used in wedding celebrations.

中华五福吉祥图典

喜

福禄寿喜财

喜
Happiness

双喜临门

Double happiness
visits the door

　　王安石赴考归途中，在与马员外女儿成亲的大喜之日，又传来金榜题名的喜讯，王安石当即书写了"囍"字，寓意双喜临门。在民俗中，结婚大喜之日，都要贴红"囍"字。喜鹊，以喜冠名，且叫声示吉兆，故以双喜鹊寓之。

　　Upon Wang Anshi's (a well-known poet of the Song Dynasty) wedding ceremony with the daughter of a distinguished official, came the announcement that he became admitted on the shortlist of royal scholars due to his excellence at exams. Thrilled, Wang wrote down the character "double happiness". In folk customs, paper-cut "double happiness" is a must for wedding decorations. Magpies are the carriers of happy messages as they have the sound of happiness in their name and signal goodness in their twitter.

◎中华五福吉祥图典

喜

福 禄 寿 喜 财

双喜临门

Double happiness at the door

官员打扮的文财神手抱珊瑚，或玉笏、如意等，另一手托"囍"。或由侍童抱一宝瓶，瓶上升起"囍"，或由侍童奉"双喜临门"的喜灯。旧时多做为门神，成双成对贴在临街的两扇门上，两位财神光临寒舍，自然是双喜临门了。

In pictures, the god of fortune in official costumes would hold coral, a jade tablet, or a *ruyi* in one hand and the character "double happiness" in the other. Alternatively, a boy accompanying him would either hold a treasure bottle with the same character erected from inside or a happiness lantern with a "double happiness at the doorstep" banner. Such images usually referred to the door god and were placed on the two doors facing the street in pairs. Double gods of fortune, double the blessings for happiness.

◎中华五福吉祥图典

喜

福 禄 寿 喜 财

喜
Happiness

双狮戏球

A pair of lions play with a ball

《宋书》："外国有狮子，威服百兽。"传统建筑门前有石狮，以镇宅驱邪。明、清时，二品武官服饰为狮。绣球，是旧时联系男女爱情的吉祥物。俗传雌雄二狮相戏时，毛缠在一起，滚而成球，小狮子便从中产出。示吉祥。

Lions, mentioned in records as animals from the west with powers above all beasts, are stationed in stone in front of traditional buildings to protect the property from evil spirits and embroidered on the costumes of military officials of the Ming and Qing dynasties, A ball made of strips of silk is a token of love. Folk-say has it that cubs are delivered from the balls of hair formed when the male and female lions play together. This is a picture of happiness and good fortune.

中华五福吉祥图典

喜

福 禄 寿 喜 财

玉镜合璧

Faithful and devoted husband and wife

《轩辕内传》："帝会王母于王屋山，铸镜十二，随月用之，此镜之始也。"相传镜为黄帝所创。因铜镜背面多铸菱花图案故在诗文中称镜子为"菱花"，李白《代美人愁镜》："在风吹却妾心断，五筋并堕菱花前。""玉镜"寓肝胆相照，"合璧"寓夫妻恩爱。

Ancient Chinese literature has it that 12 mirrors for each month of the year were first forged by the Heavenly Emperor as he met with the Heavenly Empress. A romantic name, "flower of the water chestnut" is given to mirrors in poems. Jade mirror indicates loyalty of the heart while joined pieces of jade refers to love between husband and wife.

中华五福吉祥图典

喜

福 禄 寿 喜 财

正午牡丹

The prime of prosperity

　　唐·皮日休诗："落尽残红始时芳，佳名唤作百花王。"牡丹为百花之王，花之富贵者，有国色天香之誉。正午又是牡丹盛开最娇艳之时，寓意繁荣兴旺的全盛时期。猫的眼睛随时辰而变，正午阳光最强时，猫眼缩成一条线。

　　Peony is the queen of all flowers – it is associated with riches and enjoys high prestige for its fragrance and beauty. Noon is the time of full bloom and utmost brilliance for peonies, thus a peony at noontime embodies the prime of prosperity. Also in the picture there is a cat whose eyes change with the different moments of the day and, at noon when the sun is at its strongest, cat eyes virtually turn into a line.

龙凤呈祥

Happy marriages

中华五福吉祥图典

喜

福 禄 寿 喜 财

　　龙、凤是中国古代传说中最大的神物。龙为万灵之长，是权威、尊贵的象征，视为最高男性的代表。凤是百鸟之长，是美丽、仁爱的象征，视为最高女性的代表。旧俗常把男女婚姻之喜比作"龙凤呈祥"，是对幸福的祝颂。

The dragon and the phoenix are the largest legendary animals in Chinese folklore. As the head of all living creatures, the dragon stands for authority and dignity and represents male supremacy. As the senior of all birds, the phoenix stands for beauty and love and represents female supremacy. Marriage is often described as an event of happy and fortunate combination of the dragon with the phoenix, a metaphor of sincere wishes for a good life.

喜
Happiness

龙凤呈祥

Happy marriages

龙凤呈祥，是龙凤合抱结合的吉
祥图，多用于祝贺新婚之颂词。有一
出京戏叫《龙凤呈祥》，讲的是刘备
娶孙权之妹的故事。旧时结婚贺幛
有："龙凤呈祥"、"凤翥龙翔"、"龙
腾凤翔"、"跨凤乘龙"等，多与龙凤
有关。

The happy and lucky picture where the dragon and the phoenix embrace and unite together is
often used to pay tribute to and celebrate newlyweds. A Beijing opera named Happy Union of the
Dragon and Phoenix is about an interesting anecdote: Liu Bei, a key figure of the Three King-
doms Period, married the sister of another key figure of the time, Sun Quan. In ancient times,
scrolls of congratulations for wedding occasions are
all related with the two great legendary animals –
the dragon and the phoenix.

龙生九子

The nine sons of the dragon

Designs of Chinese Blessings

明·杨慎《升庵外集》载：俗传龙生九子，各有所好：一曰贔屃，二曰螭吻，三曰蒲牢，四曰狴犴，五曰饕餮，六曰蚣蝮，七曰睚眦，八曰金猊，九曰椒图。其形象多用于古建筑或器物上。龙生九子各有其才，均成大器。

Ming Dynasty records tell about the nine sons of the dragon: all had different capabilities. Images of the nine creatures are frequently used in architecture or utensils. All nine were born with extraordinary skills and each later fulfilled significant achievements.

◎中华五福吉祥图典

喜 福 禄 寿 喜 财

喜
Happiness

平安如意

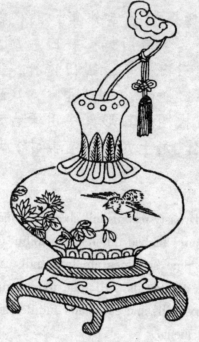

平安如意

Peace and satisfaction

《雍和宫法物说明册》："宝瓶，佛说智慧圆满具完全无漏之谓。"佛家"八吉祥"中有宝瓶，道家亦有甘露瓶。瓶的造型和命名，常取吉祥之意。"瓶"与"平"谐音，取意"平安"，瓶与如意合为：平平安安，称心如意。

In Buddhist practice, jade bottle stands for full and well-sealed wisdom and the object is one of the eight articles of fortune. The shape and name of bottles embody the concept of happiness and fortune. "Bottle" sounds the same as "peace" and "safety" in Chinese. The picture of a bottle and a *ruyi* sends a message of peace, safety, and happinesss.

◎中华五福吉祥图典

喜

福 禄 寿 喜 财

兄弟同乐

Brothers in harmony

《论语·学而》："其为人也孝弟。"尊父母为孝，敬兄长为弟。《诗经·小雅》："常棣之华，鄂不韡韡。凡今之人，莫如兄弟。"兄弟同乐、四子同乐，家和万事兴。兄弟不和则"煮豆燃豆萁，豆在釜中泣，本是同根生，相煎何太急"。

The *Analects of Confucius* emphasizes the importances of being filial to one's parents and respectful to one's elder brothers as a way of life. It also praises the beauty of harmony between brothers and that all men are but brothers. Unity, respect, and harmony within the family is the root of prosperity for each and every thing. Brothers at disaccord are like what Cao Zhi of the late Three Kingdoms Period said – beans boiled with the stems of bean vines.

◎中华五福吉祥图典

喜

福 禄 寿 喜 财

喜
Happiness

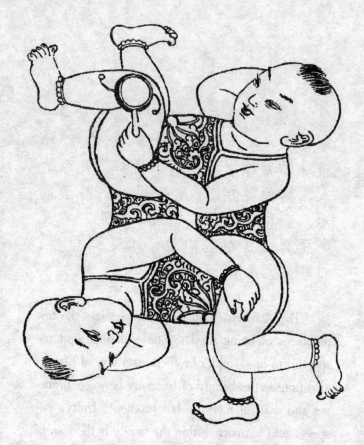

四 喜 图

Picture of four-happiness

人逢喜事精神爽，旧时曾流传这样一首《四喜诗》："久旱逢甘雨，他乡遇故知，洞房花烛夜，金榜题名时。"丰收在望、友情常在、婚姻美满、事业有成，确是人生的四大喜事。图中两个可爱的儿童，实为四童子，寓"四喜"。

One is well-refreshed when visited by good fortune such as a visible harvest, lasting friendships, happy marriage, and career achievements, just as an old four-happiness poem describes. The two lovely kids in the picture are actually four to imply four happiness.

中华五福吉祥图典

喜

福禄寿喜财

四子同乐

Four children in harmony

孔子有言曰，孝者德之本也，教之所由生也。故古帝王以孝悌治天下，而天下大治。悌者敬爱兄长，《孟子·滕文公下》："于此有人焉：入则孝，出则悌。"旧时讲多子多福，兄弟之间要团结。图中四子在抖空竹，拉地牛。

Confucius said that obedience is the essence of all merits which explains why ancient emperors relied on the rule of obedience and respect for good social order. Mencius also sang a tribute to those who were filial at home and respectful to their elder brothers outside home. Old customs value a large number of children (which brings more happiness and fortune) as well as harmony among the brothers. In the picture here, four kids are playing together happily.

中华五福吉祥图典

喜

福 禄 寿 喜 财

四喜同乐

Four children at play

"四喜同乐"是清代潍县的吉祥画，图中四个顽童在驱羊驾车，共作周游之乐。一个童子执鞭驾车，另一童子摘来一只鲜桃给车上的两位幼童。车上幼童起身欲接，另一大点幼童则恐其跌下，双手阻止，兄弟同喜同乐。

This is a picture from Wei County of the Qing Dynasty. It depicts four kids driving a cart of sheep roaming around for fun. One kid holds the whip, one other kid is handing over a freshly picked peach to the two smaller kids in the cart. In the cart, the smaller kid is just about to stand up for the peach while the bigger one gestures for him to stop, fearing that the little one might fall down. A picture of brotherly care, love, and togetherness.

四子花瓶

Flower bottles of four kids

瓶花条对是民间年画中常见的一
种形式，此图为清代亳县的窗旁。一
对双耳花瓶上插牡丹、荷花，自有平
安富贵、莲生贵子之意。瓶上画抱莲
娃各一对，旁边分衬琴、棋、书、
画。寄寓了人们希望多生子，更希望
子成才的美愿。

The picture of a pair of painted vases is a
common illustration of Chinese New Year among
common folks. And the one at hand is from a window of Bo County in the Qing Dynasty. Peonies
and lotus flowers plugged in a pair of eared bottles
indicate peace, safety, happiness, and a succession of seeds (children). Also on the bottle, a
couple of kids holding a lotus are accompanied by
a seven-stringed plucked instrument, chess, a
piece of calligraphy and painting. The picture
consigns good wishes for more children and their
great achievements in society.

仙壶集庆

Gathering at the fairy place

花瓶和水仙示"仙壶",仙壶即方壶、蓬壶、瀛洲,是仙人所居之处。蓬莱是传说中的海上仙山。李白诗《秋夕书怀》:"始探蓬壶事,旋觉天地轻。"沈亚立诗《题海榴树》:"曾在蓬壶伴众仙。""仙壶集庆"寓意众人聚会,共庆如仙。

A vase with daffodils indicates the place where the immortals reside. Many famous poets including Li Bai of the Tang Dynasty mentioned the fairy land in their works. This picture implies a happy celebration by a large gathering of people as the fairies do.

仙壶集庆

Gathering at the fairy place

《列子》：渤海东有大壑，中有五山：岱舆、员峤、方壶、瀛洲、蓬莱。五处山台是神仙居住的地方，遍地都是金玉。仙壶集庆就是仙人幽居、聚吉庆之地。以天竹谐音"祝"，以牡丹花示"富贵"，与"仙壶"合为聚仙地长寿富贵。

Ancient Chinese writings mention the place where the fairies live off the East Sea, a land of jade, gold, and lasting happiness. The image means the place the immortals, in group, live away from the madding crowd for celebration and merriment. Bamboo stands for celebration, peony flowers riches, and the vase with daffodils the gathering place of the fairies. The picture wishes for longevity and riches at the gathering place of the immortals.

中华五福吉祥图典

喜

福 禄 寿 喜 财

瓜瓞绵绵

Lasting generations
of offsprings

大瓜、小瓜累累，结在绵长的藤蔓之上，表示世代绵长，子孙万代。《诗·大雅·绵》："绵绵瓜瓞，民之初生，自土沮漆。"《疏》："大者曰瓜，小者曰瓞。"讲的是周朝的先祖像瓜瓞一样代代相传，到周文王才奠定了王业基础。

Melons growing on long vines are a sign of lasting generations of offsprings. The picture originates from ancient literature and gives an account of the long and succeeding generations of the ancestors of the Zhou Dynasty as its foundation was finally formed during the reign of King Wen of Zhou.

◎中华五福吉祥图典

喜 福 禄 寿 喜 财

兰室评梅

Appreciating plum flowers
in the orchid room

腊月寒尽，梅花初开，兰室之
内，一贵妇人身披轻裘，下系皮裙，
坐于凳上品茶消闲。另一扎髻之少
女，手拿一瓶梅花似在邀赏品评。关
于梅的品格，旧时有"四德"之说：
"梅具四德，初生为元，开花如亨，
结子为利，成熟为贞。"

At the end of the cold months of the year
when plum blossoms are blooming, a noble woman
in beautiful clothes is enjoying tea in an orchid
room. A young girl holding a bottle of plum blossoms appears to be inviting the lady to appraise the
flowers. Four virtues are to be cited on the person-
ality of plum blossoms: vitality at birth, prosperity
at bloom, luck and fortune at seed-bearing, and
integrity in adulthood.

兰闺韵事

兰闺韵事

*A colorful life
of young women*

敞轩兰室，绣幔高卷，户外花草
舒风，芭蕉展绿，室内五位美女在吟
诗作画。图中一女子在展卷吟诗，另
一女子坐于画案前，挥毫弄丹青。其
余女子，或轻轻扶纸，或静静欣赏。
描写了佳丽兰闺多韵事，才女作画又
吟诗。

In a spacious and bright orchid room located
in a pleasant environment, five beautiful and tal-
ented women are enjoying a life of various interesting themes – one is composing a poem, another is
drawing a picture, and the rest are lending a help-
ing hand or just quietly enjoying themselves.

◎中华五福吉祥图典

喜

褔 禄 寿 喜 财

母子同乐

Joy shared by mother and child

線 臨

"慈母手中线，游子身上衣，临
行密密缝，意恐迟迟归，谁言寸草
心，报得三春晖。"《游子吟》是唐朝
颂扬母子之情的诗。《母子同乐》是
清朝歌颂母子之情的画。旗装妇女拉
二胡，扎辫男童击手磬，描绘出新年
时母子欢乐情景。

A Tang poem known to almost all Chinese
people praises the love a mother has for her son
who is about to embark on a voyage to a far-away
place. Joy Shared by Mum and Son is a picture
that pays tribute to love between mother and son in
the Qing Dynasty. The woman in a banner-man at-
tire is playing *erhu* while her son in braids is beat-
ing the chime stone. A happy scene around the
time of Chinese New Year.

◎中华五福吉祥图典

喜

福 禄 寿 喜 财

喜
Happiness

吉光高照

The light of luck and

happiness shines over

———— 074

《易·系辞上》："吉，无不利。"《易·系辞下》："吉事有祥。"《庄子》："虚室生日，吉祥止止。" 《注疏》："吉者福善之事，祥者嘉庆之征。"吉者，吉利、吉祥也。吉光高照。可使家庭安乐、人丁兴旺、国家昌盛、天下太平。

Chinese literature from very ancient times has described 吉 (*jí*) as associated with fortune, good luck, and generally good things. Where the light of fortune shines above, a household is guaranteed to enjoy peace and prosperity; likewise, a country blessed by lights of fortune is sure to be thriving and tranquil.

◎中华五福吉祥图典

喜

福 禄 寿 喜 财

吉庆如意

Happiness, celebration, and satisfaction

磬，是古代宫廷的打击乐器，多由灵璧石制成。古磬有两种：悬一面独奏者为"持磬"，悬多面合奏者为"编磬"。制磬的灵璧石也称磬石，声音清亮悦耳。在这幅母子对屏中，挂在如意上的磬和挂在珊瑚上的如意，合为吉庆如意。

Chime stone is an ancient royal percussion musical instrument often made of stone. The sound this chime stone makes is clear and very pleasant. In this picture of mothers and sons, the chime stone hung on the *ruyi* and the *ruyi* hung on the coral combine to mean happiness, celebration, and the state of being well-contented.

中华五福吉祥图典

喜

福 禄 寿 喜 财

喜

Happiness

吉祥万年

*Lasting happiness
and good fortune*

◎中华五福吉祥图典

　　万年青，意为万年长青，被视为吉祥之物。《花镜》："吴中人家多种之，造屋易居，行聘治圹，小儿初生，一切喜事，无不用之，以为祥瑞口号。""象"与"祥"谐音，佛之"卐"字与"万"也谐音，合为"吉祥万年"，寓吉祥长久。

　　The rohdea japonica tree means ever green and is thus seen as an object of happiness and fortune. It is recorded that this tree is frequently used as an auspicious sign for such happy family events as house building, change of residence, marriage proposal, etc. "Elephant" is the same in sound as "luck" while the Buddhist sign 卐 is the same in sound as 10,000 . Jointly in this picture, the visuals mean lasting happiness and fortune.

喜

福 禄 寿 喜 财

吉祥万年

Lasting happiness and good fortune

在中国传统文化中，象被视为吉祥嘉瑞，是太平盛世的瑞应物。《春秋运斗枢》："摇光之星散为象。"《宋书·符瑞志》："象车者，山之精也，王者德泽流洽四境则出。""象车"是政清民和、天下太平之祥瑞，象又喻"吉祥"。

In traditional Chinese culture, the elephant is a symbol of fortune and good luck, and signals prosperity and tranquility. Ancient Chinese literature associates the elephant with the moralistic ruling of the emperor. It stands for clean governance, unity of the people, and a peaceful world.

喜
Happiness

吉祥如意

*Happiness, good fortune,
and satisfaction*

《稗史类篇》："如意者，古之爪杖也，或用竹木，削作人手指爪，柄可长三尺许。或背脊有痒，手不到，用以抓搔，如人之意。"如意原为古时的搔杖，后成为供观赏的吉祥物。图以"象"示"祥"，"吉祥如意"意为吉庆祥瑞尽随人意。

It is recorded that *ruyi* actually started as a stick of wood or bamboo with finger-like top to scratch one's back where the hand fails to reach; it serves to ease the itching to one's heart's content. *Ruyi* evolved to become a lucky object for display and appreciation. With the elephant standing for "luck", the picture means happiness, fortune, and to the full content of the heart.

喜
Happiness

芒种报春

The Mang god announces the arrival of spring

《礼记》："孟春三月，其神句
芒。"芒神又叫"句芒"，为春神。
《山海经》："东方句芒，鸟身人面，
乘两龙。"民间年画中有"春牛图"，
画芒神与黄牛来表示春之将及，宜为
农事早作准备。图中芒神穿仙衣，吹
横笛，背倚卧牛。

Ancient Chinese records tell people that the
god of spring is named Mang. It is further recorded that this god riding on two dragons had the body
of a bird and the face of a man and Chinese New
Year common folk pictures depict spring scenes
with images of the Mang god and an ox, indicating
spring is approaching and farming preparations
should be made. In these pictures, the Mang god
wears fairy clothes, plays a flute, and leans a-
gainst a lying ox.

◎中华五福吉祥图典

喜

福 禄 寿 喜 财

百子同欢

100 *joyful children*

旧时，门神画多贴在临街大门上，而门童画多贴在院内屋门上，画的多是吉祥娃娃画也称"金童子"。此图与下图为一对"门童"，过节时贴于屋门之上，以求"多子多福"、"百子百福"、"多子多孙"、"子孙万代"之福。

In traditional Chinese customs, the god of the gate is often posted on the gate facing the street while door-god is usually seen on doors inside the yard. The latter features kids representing good fortune and are thus also called golden kids. This picture and the picture after this form a pair of door kid pictures. They are posted on doors during festivals to wish for more children and more luck.

中华五福吉祥图典

喜 福 禄 寿 喜 财

喜
Happiness

百子同喜

100 joyful children

Designs of Chinese Blessings

中国以百言其多，故有"百福图"、"百寿图"、百子图"等。有男子、有多子、有百子，是家中大福，故旧时"百子图"很受人们欢迎。在"百子图"中，有的则画一百个百态嬉戏的可爱孩童，有的则以"多子"代"百子"。

In China 100 is a figure that represents plenty which tells why pictures like "100 kinds of good fortune", "100 years of longevity", and "100 children" are so popular. It is the great fortune of the household to have male offspring and to have many children. In some of these pictures there are as many as 100 children.

中华五福吉祥图典

喜

福 禄 寿 喜 财

百子嬉戏

100 children at play

旧时，有的百子图上还有题诗。如："麟趾祯祥瑞气和，乃生男子祝三多，衍庆螽斯载弄璋，世称百子颂欢呼。"图中有的童子在弹琴、下棋、读书、画画，有的在舞狮，还有的在放风筝……。表现了儿童天真无邪的游戏。

In the past, pictures of 100 children may even have poems to go with them. The picture gives a full and vivid illustration of lovely and naive children enjoying games of their age such as playing with a musical instrument, chess, reading, drawing, lion dance, or kite flying.

喜
Happiness

百子百孙

100 children and grandchildren

Designs of Chinese Blessings

　　旧俗过春节时，常贴百子百孙图，并有对联贴于门上："一门五福陈箕范；四代同堂庆瓞绵。"生育繁衍，是人类得以传代的必需。旧时，儿孙满堂是老一辈的福分，多子多嗣是晚一辈的孝顺。百子百孙，家族兴旺。

　　In old customs, pictures of 100 children are posted to celebrate the Chinese New Year festival. Also appearing on the doors is a poem that wishes the household prosperity with all the blessings it can get and abundance and continuity in offspring. To bear children and multiply is a necessity for mankind to continue itself. To the older generation, it is good fortune to have a full household of children and grandchildren; to the younger generation, to have a large family is their demonstration of filial piety. Many children and grandchildren indicate the household will be prosperous.

◎中华五福吉祥图典

喜

福 禄 寿 喜 财

百年和合

Harmony and love for 100 years

百合花，姿香俱佳，且名吉祥，取其"百"与"和"。万年青，经冬不凋，为吉祥之物，取其"年"。荷花，出污泥而不染，花中之君子，取其"合"。种荷花之盒，也取其"合"。百合、万年青、荷花、盒子，四种吉祥物组成"百年和合"，以祝新婚。

Lilies, which bear a lucky name in Chinese, are outstanding both in their looks and fragrance. Rondea japonica bears auspicious signs as it does not wither during the winter. Lotus is the gentleman of flowers as it grows from mud and remains unspoiled. The box the lotus is planted in carries the sound of "harmony" in Chinese. These four mascots are put together to wish the newlyweds harmony and love for 100 years.

◎中华五福吉祥图典

喜

福 禄 寿 喜 财

喜
Happiness

百事大吉

Fortunate and smooth in all things

百合示"百"，柿子谐音"事"，大桔子谐音"大吉"，合为"百事大吉"。百为多、为极。大为宽、为广、为高、为厚。百事大吉即事事大吉大利。另图以柏树谐音"百"，以灵芝仙草代"如意"，合为"百事如意"。多作颂辞。

Lilies stand for 100, which means a lot and to the extreme, persimmons refer to things, large oranges sound the same as "extremely fortunate", and the three combine to mean immensely fortunate in everything. Other images also use cypress for 100 and glossy ganoderma for heart-content and jointly mean to the full content of the heart in all things. Both are eulogies.

百事如意

To the heart's full content

in each and every thing

百合花色彩艳丽，花姿绰约，盛
开夏日，其名吉祥，以寓其"百"。
百为极数，言其多。图中女人手中的
"柿"，童子拉的"狮"，谐音"事"。
另一女子手持如意，合为"百事如
意"。一事如意易，百事称心如意是
人们的美好愿望。

Lilies, in full bloom during summer, are
bright in color and graceful in posture besides a
lucky name which bears the sound of 100. 100
means a lot and to the extreme. In the picture,
the persimmon the woman holds in her hand and
the lion the child is pulling both share the sound
of "things". Another girl holds a *ruyi* in her
hand. All these combine to mean to one's heart's
full content in each and every thing. Whereas it is
an easy thing to get one thing done to one's satisfaction, it is hard to get all things that way. The
picture here serves as a well-intended wish of people.

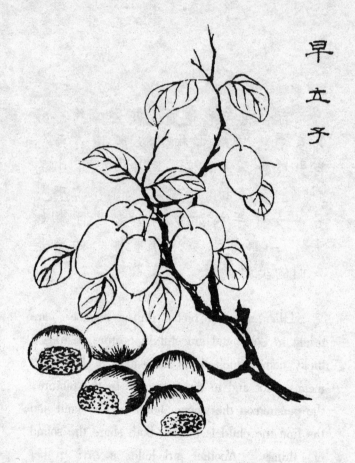

早立子

早立子

To bear children at an early date

《礼记·曲礼》："妇人之贽，脯修枣栗也。"《国语》："夫妇贽不过枣栗，以告虔也。"《注》："枣取早起，栗取欲栗，虔敬也。"枣与栗合，在古代用以表示妇人之贽。"枣"谐"早"，"栗子"谐"立子"，早立子源于中国传统观念"早生儿子早得济"。

Ancient Chinese writings record that the initial gifts a married woman receives should be properly dates and chestnuts as a pious wish that she will bear children at her new home at an early date. As dates read "early" and chestnut "child bearing" in Chinese pronunciation, the choice of such gifts conforms to the Chinese traditional concept that she who gets children early reaps the benefits therein early as well.

中华五福吉祥图典

喜

福禄寿喜财

同　喜

Happiness to you as well

旧时，当接受别人贺喜时，往往以"同喜"作答。喜鹊在古代曾被称作神女，有预兆先知的神异本领。民间也将喜鹊作为喜鸟，在吉祥图中多表示"喜"。梧桐自古就被认为是中国的吉祥树，相传梧桐有圣洁之身，故凤凰只落此树，"桐"谐"同"。

A proper response to congratulations under the old customs is to say "happiness to you as well". Magpies are considered prophets in old times as well as messengers of good news. In pictures celebrating happy events, the bird stands for happiness. Chinese parasol trees have since ancient times been seen as symbols of happiness and good fortune. Legend has it that the trees are holy and pure and are the only kind of trees a phoenix would rest on. The tree bears the same sound as "also".

因 和 得 偶

Kind temperament brings
good companions

宋·米友仁《临江仙》："溪上新荷初出水，花房半弄微红。"金·蔡松年《鹧鸪天·赏荷》："胭脂雪瘦薰沉水，翡翠盘高走夜光。"荷叶碧绿如翠，莲藕洁白似玉，因荷得偶。"荷"谐"和"，"藕"谐"偶"因和得偶寓意因和善而得佳偶。

Many beautiful poems are dedicated to the green lotus leaves and the pure and white lotus roots beneath. Lotus shares the sound of "harmony" and lotus root the sound of "companion" so the two join to mean one gets good companion owing to one's kind temperament.

中华五福吉祥图典

喜

福 禄 寿 喜 财

喜
Happiness

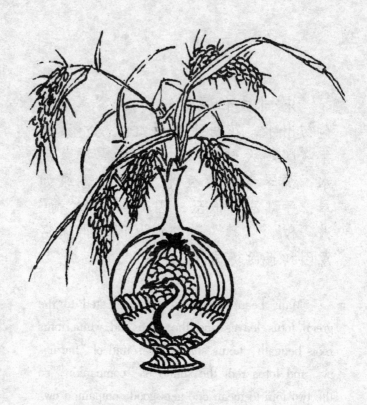

岁岁平安

Peace year after year

Designs of Chinese Blessings

《诗·王风·黍离》："彼稷之穗。"
张祜《经旧游》诗："水溅花穗倒空
潭。"穗，是谷类花实结聚成的长条。
多个穗，果实累累，取其音表示"岁
岁"。鹤纹瓶表示"平安"之意。在
旧时辞旧迎新之际，多以岁岁平安、
年年如意作颂辞。

Ears of grain are the long strings of cereal
seeds at maturity and the more of them, the better
a harvest. "Many ears of grain" share the sound of
"year after year" while the crane-lined bottle
stands for peace and safety. In ancient times,
when people bid goodbye to the old year and
greeting a new year, peace and content year after
year is an eulogy that suits the occasion perfectly.

喜
Happiness

岁岁平安

Peace year after year

王安石《元日》诗："爆竹声中一岁除，春风送暖入屠苏。千门万户曈曈日，总把新桃换旧符。"旧时春节，人们燃放爆竹以送旧迎新。传说"年"为妖，每年岁末出来祸害人畜，民以爆竹驱"年"，此风俗延袭至今，以求岁岁平安。

As the Song poet Wang Anshi said in his poem, firecrackers are blown to send away the old year and a spring breeze blows in a new season, an occasion to replace the old peach wood charms and couplet with new ones. Legend has it that "year" is a demon and must be driven away with firecrackers at the end of the year when it customarily comes out to harm people. Such practice has been followed till this day to seek peace year on year.

中华五福吉祥图典

喜

福 禄 寿 喜 财

年年大吉

Great fortune year after year

鲶鱼，亦称鲇，身体前部平扁，后部侧扁，大者长达一米多，灰黑色有暗色斑块。口宽大有须两对，眼小无鳞，皮肤富粘液腺，肉味美。"鲶"谐"年"，"桔"谐"吉"。两条鲶鱼为"年年"，大桔子为"大吉"。祝愿年年大吉是旧时春节颂辞。

Catfish, also groupers, which can grow to be one meter in length, are gray fish with dark spots. A pair of beard grow next to the broad mouth. They have small eyes, wear no scales, and are very delicious. "Catfish" shares the same pronunciation with "year" while "orange" shares the same with "good fortune". Two catfish and a large orange, meaning great fortune year after year, form an eulogy for the Chinese New Year.

◎中华五福吉祥图典

喜

福 禄 寿 喜 财

喜
Happiness

年年大吉

Great fortune year after year

鲶鱼之"鲶"谐音"年",两条鲶鱼示"年年"。"桔"与"吉"谐音,大桔示"大吉"。合为"年年大吉"。桔为吉祥物,据历史记载,宋朝时只有皇后才能食金桔。《春秋运斗枢》:"旋星散为桔。"在吉祥图中多以"桔"喻"吉"。

"Catfish" shares the same pronunciation with "year" and two catfish together mean year on year. "Orange" shares the same pronunciation with "good fortune" and a large orange means extremely good fortune. The objects combined mean great fortune year after year. As an object of good fortune, historical records say that in the Song Dynasty, only the empress was permitted to eat gold oranges which explains why oranges are often used to mean good fortune in images of good luck.

◎中华五福吉祥图典

喜

福 禄 寿 喜 财

年年如意

Full content to the heart
year on year

如意，是中国传统的吉祥物。长不过一二尺，其端多作芝形、云形，材多为竹、木、牙、角、金、玉等，以供赏玩。鲶鱼，肉美，鳔可入药。"鲶"与"年"谐音，两条鲶鱼示"年年"图中的云纹示如意。合为年年如意、岁岁平安。

Ruyi is a mascot in Chinese tradition. Just about one or two feet long, it is made of bamboo, wood, ivory, horn, gold, or jade and often in the shape of clouds or glossy ganoderma at the ends. Catfish is a delicacy. "Catfish" shares the same pronunciation with "year" and two catfish together means year on year. The cloud shape in the visual evokes a *ruyi*. In combination, the message is full content to the heart year on year and peace and tranquility at all time.

中华五福吉祥图典

◎

喜

福 禄 寿 喜 财

竹报平安

Explosion of firecrackers brings along peace

古代在佳节喜庆之日，用火烧竹，爆裂发声，称为"爆竹"。传说能驱除山鬼。后以多层纸密裹火药，接以药线，点燃即爆。王安石《元日》诗云："爆竹声中一岁除。""爆"谐音报，"竹报平安"意为驱除邪恶，祈盼平安。

In ancient times, during festivals and celebrations people would burn bamboo sticks with fire to hear the cracking sound the sticks make as they break, they called these firecrackers. Legend has it that the firecrackers serve to drive away evil spirits. Later, the sticks evolved to be powder wrapped in layers of paper with a twist thread and explode when ignited. As Wang Anshi put it, a year goes by with the sound of firecrackers. The explosion of firecrackers brings peace along. The picture means to drive away evil spirits and wish for peace and safety.

◎中华五福吉祥图典

喜

福 禄 寿 喜 财

喜
Happiness

竹报平安

竹报平安

Explosion of firecrackers
brings along peace

《谈闻录》载：古代有一叫年的怪兽，每年腊月三十出来伤人。一次"年"在村庄中遇两牧童甩鞭，啪啪的响声把"年"吓跑。以后每到"年"出来时，就燃放爆竹以求平安。图中以童子手中的竹示"竹报"，以花瓶示"平安"。

Records tell that there was a beast called "year" in ancient times that came out to harm people every year on December 30 lunar calendar. Once "year" met two shepherd boys in the village who blew their whip at it; frightened, "year" ran away. Later on, whenever it was time for "year" to come, firecrackers were burned to beg for peace and safety. The bamboo stick in the hand of the boy stands for "firecrackers explode" and the flower bottle means "peace and safety".

竹梅双喜

*Naïve young lovers grow
up to be life companions*

中华五福吉祥图典

　　李白《长干行》诗："郎骑竹马
来，绕床弄青梅。同居长干里，两小
无嫌猜。"后来用"青梅竹马"形容
男女儿童天真无邪，在一起玩耍。
"竹梅双喜"即两小无猜，长大结为
伴侣，夫妻恩爱、婚姻美满。以竹、
梅、喜鹊喻之。

　　In one of his famous poems, Li Bai described
a neighboring young boy and girl who shared an
innocent and naive friendship. Bamboo horses and
green plums mentioned in the poem later evolved
to refer to innocent little boys and girls playing
games together. When bamboo, plums, and magpies are placed together in this picture, it means
that the naive young girl and boy, after sharing a
happy childhood, grew up to be companions for
life and united in a happy marriage.

喜

福 禄 寿 喜 财

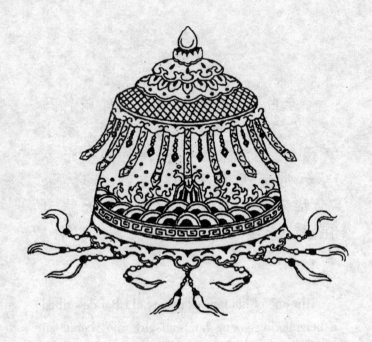

华盖祥兆

Good luck under the

imperial canopy

华盖，亦称宝盖，是帝王或高官显贵所用的伞形遮蔽物。华盖之下必有吉祥。崔豹《古今注·舆服》："华盖，黄帝所作也，与蚩尤战于涿鹿之野，常有五色气，金枝玉叶，止于帝上，有花葩之象，故因而作华盖也。"

An canopy over an imperial carriage is sure to bring good luck. Record has it that when the Yellow Emperor fought with Chiyou in the fields, over his carriage there were clouds of five colors, gold and jade tree leaves stayed over, and flowers appeared. So the canopy implies good luck.

中华五福吉祥图典

喜

福 禄 寿 喜 财

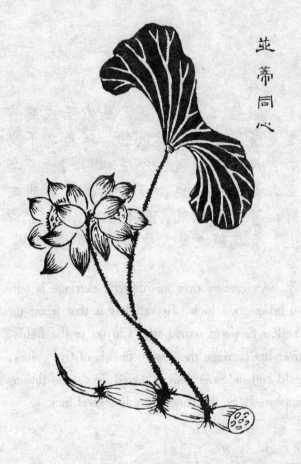

並蒂同心

并蒂同心

Double lotus flowers share
the same heart

《花镜》："并头莲红白俱有，一干两花。"在百花中，唯莲能花、果、子并存。一茎双花的并蒂莲，是纯真爱情的象征，也是人寿年丰的预兆。《留鞋记》："休拗折并头莲，莫捻杀双飞燕。""并蒂同心"寓夫妻恩爱、心心相印。

Among all the flowers, the lotus is the only one that has its flowers, fruits and seeds on the same plant. Two lotus flowers on one stem is the symbol of pure love as well as an auspicious sign of longevity and good harvest. People are persuaded not to snap double lotus flowers or to kill two flying swallows. "Double lotus flowers share the same heart" consigns that husband and wife are affectionate toward each other and share telesthesia.

◎中华五福吉祥图典

喜

福 禄 寿 喜 财

安居乐业

Peaceful life and happy work

《后汉书·仲长统传》："安居乐业，长养子孙，天下晏然，皆归心于我矣。"《汉书·货殖传》："各安其居而乐其业，甘其食而美其服。"以鹌鹑之"鹌"谐"安"，以"菊"谐"居"，枫树为落叶乔木，以"落叶"谐"乐业"。形容安定生活，愉快劳动。

In traditional Chinese culture, much significance is attached to the concept of common people enjoying their lives and taking delight in what they do for a living. It is well conceived to the leaders of the country that the implementation of such a concept is essential to a peaceful nation and loyal people. In this picture, "quails" sound the same as "peaceful", "chrysanthemums" sound the same as "living", and "fallen leaves" sound the same as "enjoy one's work". The message the picture sends is that people enjoy a peaceful life and work happily.

◎中华五福吉祥图典

喜

福 禄 寿 喜 财

喜
Happiness

安居乐业

Peaceful and self-contented life

安居乐业源于《老子》："甘其食，美其服，安其俗，乐其业。邻国相望，鸡犬之声相闻，民至老死，不相往来。"安居乐业，是指社会生活安定，人们乐于工作，精神、物质生活丰富。而老子讲的是"老死不相往来"的安居乐业。

To enjoy one's life and take delight in what one does for a living originated from the works of Laozi. Laozi envisioned a society where the people were so contented with their lives, clothes, customs, and work that they had no communication at all with their neighboring state till death even though they were just a stone's throw away. The concept now mainly emphasizes the abundance of spiritual and material life in a peaceful society.

◎中华五福吉祥图典

喜 福 禄 寿 喜 财

观音送子

The Goddess of Mercy sends
over children

观音是佛国诸菩萨之首，观世音来到中国后，久而久之被汉化，在妇女心目中对观音的崇拜超过了佛祖。观音菩萨以慈悲为怀，普渡众生，无所不能。于是人们又给她加上了一个"送子"功能，这也符合观音有多种化身。

The Goddess of Mercy, the head of all Bodhisattvas in Buddhism, gradually adapted to the local conditions of China after it was introduced in the county. Chinese women worshipped the Goddess of Mercy more than they did the Buddha as the former is compassionate and able to do all things to help the vast populace. To complement its multiple incarnations, the function of child-sending has been added to it.

喜
Happiness

白衣大士送子觀音

送子观音

*The Goddess of Mercy sends
over children*

132

由于中国长久的"多子"观念，所以送子神仙也多。如：王母娘娘、天妃娘娘、九天玄女、碧霞元君，以及送子观音、送子张仙等。旧时无后的妇女，到观音庙偷拿供奉的莲灯，"灯"与"丁"谐音，借得观音莲灯，家中自会"添丁"。

In line with the long-cherished value of "having lots of children", lots of fairies are deemed to have the function of "child-sending" in old China. The Heavenly Empress, and the child-sending Goddess of Mercy for example. In old customs, women with no children would go and steal home the lotus lanterns offered to the Goddess of Mercy. As "lantern" shares the same pronunciation as "family member", the lantern would surely bless the household and help them add number to their people.

中华五福吉祥图典

喜 福 禄 寿 喜 财

喜 Happiness

多子多福

More children, more good fortune

　　儿孙满堂、世代绵延，是古人人生的第一事业。多男子，是家庭的福分。图中的石榴，果实"多子"。佛手的"佛"谐音"福"，与童子手中的蝙蝠，为"多福"。另童子怀抱的大寿桃，以及仙鹤，为"多寿"，也有"三多"之意。

To have children and grandchildren all over the house and continuous generations of offsprings is the number one business in life for ancient Chinese people. It is good fortune to have lots of male members. Pomegranate is a fruit of many seeds and serves to evoke a lot of children in the picture. Bergamot shares the same pronunciation as "happiness" and joins with the bat in the hand of the boy to mean a lot of happiness. The large birthday peach held by the boy and the crane combine to mean great longevity.

◎中华五福吉祥图典

喜

福　禄　寿　喜　财

欢天喜地

Overwhelmingly happy

獾

元·王实甫《西厢记》："则见他欢天喜地，谨依来命。"獾，亦称猪獾，头长耳短，前肢特长，善于掘土，通常筑洞于土丘或大树下，洞道甚长。"獾"与"欢"谐音，喜鹊有"喜"。喜鹊翔于天而看地，獾立于地而望天，为"欢天喜地"。

The phrase overwhelmingly happy came from a play of the Yuan Dynasty. Badgers, long-headed and short-eared with long arms, are good at excavating earth. They would dig long holes under large trees or hillocks. Badgers share the same pronunciation with "happiness" while magpie has the word "happiness" in its name. A magpie is flying in the air and looking down, a badger is standing on the ground and looking up, hence happy in heaven and earth – which now means overwhelmingly happy.

中华五福吉祥图典

喜

福 禄 寿 喜 财

Happiness

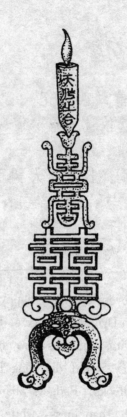

欢爱烛红

Red candles celebrating marital love

Designs of Chinese Blessings

"欢爱洞房红烛夜，良辰美景新婚时"。旧时，新婚洞房要点上红蜡烛，以贺新婚之喜。图中磬上有囍，为喜庆之意，并有祥云缭绕。囍上有寿，寿上有元宝，宝之上是"天作之合"的红蜡烛。此图为民间新婚时用的窗花纹样。

Old customs require a pair of red candles be lit and placed in the bedroom of new couples as a form of congratulations. The chime stone, clouds, the words double happiness and longevity, and the shoe-shaped gold ingots all carry meanings of luck, happiness, and congratulations. The visual is often used in paper-cut for window decoration for newlyweds of the common folks.

中华五福吉祥图典

喜 福 禄 寿 喜 财

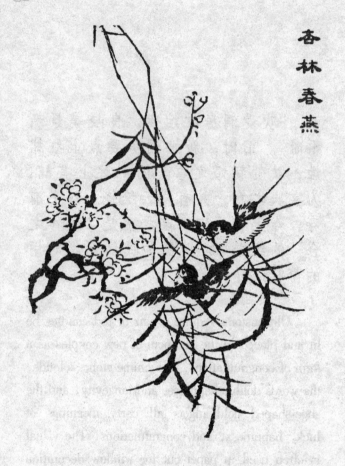

杏林春燕

杏林春燕

Spring swallows amongst
apricot woods

《神仙传》载：相传三国时吴人董奉为人治病，不受报酬，对治愈的病人，只求为其种几株杏树。数年后竟得杏树十余万株，蔚然成林。后世常以杏林春燕、杏林春满、誉满杏林等语称颂医家。也是对德高望重、多行好义之士的赞誉。

It was recorded that during the Three King-doms Period, a guy named Dong Feng offered to treat illness for people without charging any fee. Those who got cured were only required to plant a few apricot trees. Several years later, the number of apricot trees grew to be over a hundred thousand and an apricot forest appeared. Later, phrases such as spring swallows amongst apricot woods have evolved to be eulogies for doctors. They also serve as praises for highly respected and generous people.

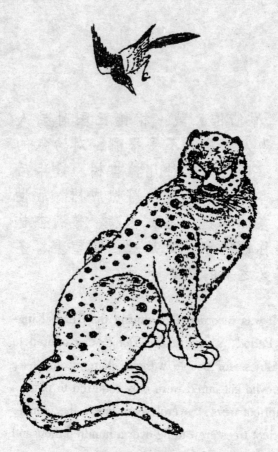

报 喜 图

Announcement of happy news

《说文》："豹，似虎，环文。"豹示英武，清朝三品武官服饰豹。古代以"豹尾"象征爵禄、荣誉。称用兵之术为"豹韬"。图中以"豹"谐音"报"，并取喜鹊之"喜"，合为"报喜图"。喜鹊是报喜的吉祥鸟，人见人爱。

Leopards are animals of bravery and leopard images were worn by Qing military officials on their costumes. In the past, leopard tail referred to wages and honor and military art was called leopard strategies. In the picture, leopard shares the same pronunciation as "announcement" and, combined with the "happiness" sound in magpies, means announcement of happy news. As birds of good luck that bring good news, magpies are darling birds.

中华五福吉祥图典

喜

福 禄 寿 喜 财

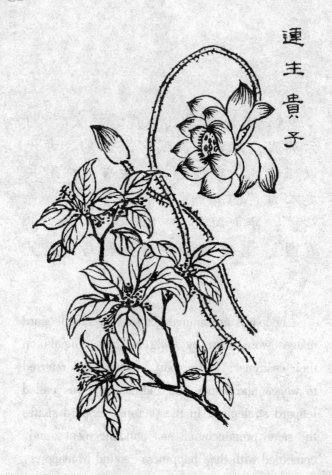

連生貴子

连生贵子

To have children one after another

桂花=贵也
莲生贵子

汉·刘向《说苑·谈丛》："庶人将昌，必有良子。"明·冯梦龙《警世通言·宋小官团圆破毡笠》："养儿待老，积谷防饥。"宋·苏轼："无官一身轻，有子万事足。"图以莲花、桂花谐音喻之。多生子、生贵子是旧时家中大喜事。

A son or child in the household provides for family prosperity and is the necessary provision for one's old age just as grains are stored for times of famine. Su Shi of the Song Dynasty said in his poem that he felt light with no official title and was content with life now that he had a child. In old times, to have a lot of children and boys in particular was an event of great happiness for the household. Lotus flowers and sweet-scented osmanthuses in the picture share the same pronunciation with "having children in succession".

喜
Happiness

连生贵子

To have children one after another

146

早生贵子、多生贵子、连生贵子，旧时以"多子"为内容的吉祥图很多。图中童子吹笙，谐音"生"，莲谐音"连"，莲子谐音"子"合为"连生贵子"。旧时生子有送联之习，联句如："子种莲房多多益善，梦延瓜瓞久久长绵。"

A lot of ancient pictures featuring good luck are about the theme of children – have children at an early age, bear a lot of children, and have children consecutively. In the picture here, a child is playing *xiao*, a musical instrument bearing the sound of "smile". Lotus flowers bear the sound of "succession" whereas lotus seeds "children". The visuals combine to mean to have children one after another. In old customs, couplets are given at childbirth with words congratulating on the event and wishing the family to go on generation after generation.

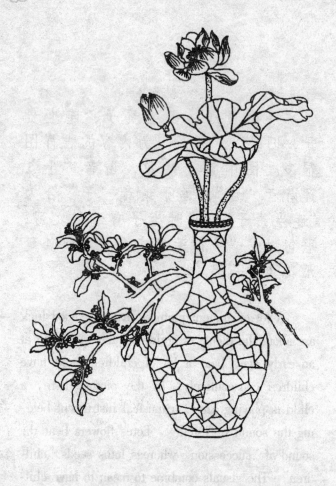

连生贵子

*To have children
one after another*

生子是家中大事，古礼生子三日，要设汤饼宴客，俗称吃"三朝酒"。儿子周岁时要"试周"，即在盘中装上玩具，让儿子选择以试前途。传说宋代曹彬，试周时左手拿干戈，右手取祭器，后又取印一颗，曹彬长大做官果成将相。

Childbirth is a big event for a family. According to old rites on the third day after the delivery, the family would give a banquet serving soup and cake. Upon the first birthday of the child, a test was held to foretell its future where all kinds of things would be placed together and people could see what the child took to its hands. Anecdote says that a well-known general of the Song Dynasty took a weapon, a sacrificial utensil, and a seal. And he turned out to be a famous general when he grew up.

中华五福吉祥图典

喜 福 禄 寿 喜 财

連生貴子

连生贵子

To have children
one after another

　　"连生贵子"也称"莲生贵子",
吉祥图中"连"多以"莲"谐音,故
直取"莲"字。图中以花架上的大盆
莲花喻之。三位活泼可爱的童子,年
龄相差不多,也有"贵子连生"之
意。由于连生贵子,故三位妇女优闲
自得,生活充满乐趣。

　　As lotus flowers share the sound of "succession", a large pot of lotus flowers is placed in the
picture. The three lovely kids are about the same
age. And the mothers of the three kids, having
accomplished a lot for their families, are looking
relaxed and appreciate the rewards of life.

中华五福吉祥图典

喜

福 禄 寿 喜 财

听好消息

Good tidings come in

以捉鬼而闻名民间的钟馗，其画像大多面目狰狞，是辟邪除恶的护家神。以捉鬼驱邪为专职的钟馗，虽面目丑陋，却颇受人们的欢迎，渐渐地也被奉为迎祥纳福的吉祥之神。钟馗吹笛，绕梁三日传来佳信，引来福音。

Zhong Kui, established himself among the common folks as the house guardian against evil spirits, often appears ugly and frightening in pictures. Though unpleasant in appearance, Zhong Kui is a popular figure as he sees it his exclusive responsibilities to drive away evil spirits. Gradually, he has become the god of good fortune. As he plays the flute, the music stays round the house for three days, bringing over good tidings.

中华五福吉祥图典

喜 福 禄 寿 喜 财

事事如意

To the heart's content in everything

◎中华五福吉祥图典

喜

福 禄 寿 喜 财

事事如意，寓事事吉祥如意。传统图案中用"柿"谐音"事"，两个柿子为"事事"。如意，柄端原作手指状，用以搔痒可如人意，故而得名。后柄渐渐缩短加粗，将前端改为灵芝形或祥云形，造型更加优美，成为供观赏的吉祥物。

In traditional patterns, persimmons are used for their similarity to "thing" in sound. Double persimmons mean "everything". *Ruyi* comes from a stick with finger-like top to scratch on the back where the hand fails to reach; it serves to ease the itching to one's heart's content. Later on, the handle gradually becomes thicker and shorter with its top turned into shape of auspicious clouds or glossy ganodermas. It later turned more artistic in looks for display and appreciation.

155

喜 *Happiness*

堂 满

和气满堂

Thorough modesty and gentleness

156

厅堂之上，两个头簪翠花，身穿百褶裙，宽领大袖袍的清装妇女，一抱爱犬，一拿纨扇坐立其后。可爱的童子手捧宝瓶，上插荷花，以"荷"谐"和"，寓意全家欢乐，和气满堂。谦和，是人与人之间友好的纽带，为人处世要待人谦和。

In the main hall are two women with beautiful Qing clothes and accessories – one carrying a pet dog, the other sitting behind with a silk fan in her hand. A lovely kid holds a bottle with lotus flowers in. Lotus flowers mean "harmony" in sound, hinting life in the family is happy, harmonious, and full of friendly feelings. Modesty and gentleness are the friendly ties between people and rules of thumb in bearing oneself.

◎中华五福吉祥图典

喜 福 禄 寿 喜 财

和气致祥

Good luck induced
by harmonious relations

阿福，是民间尤其是南方流行的泥塑。阿福个头不高，体态丰腴，端庄质朴。慈眉善目，面含微笑，和蔼可亲。身着金线牡丹袍，手捧"和气致祥"的横幅，浑身上下充满着和气。旧时买卖人讲究和气生财，和气可带来吉祥。

Afu is a mud statue popular among common people, especially in south China. Afu is short and stout in shape and wears an elegant yet unpretending expression. He looks very kind and amiable with a pleasant smile on his face. Wearing a gold-threaded peony gown he holds a banner in his hands saying "kindness above all" which presents him as the very symbol of friendly feelings. In old customs, merchants valued kindness highly as fortune was believed to be induced by harmonious relations.

◎中华五福吉祥图典

喜

福 禄 寿 喜 财

和合二仙

The two gods of harmony

和合之神，原是唐朝的万回。到明末清初，被寒山与拾得二人取代。寒山手捧一盒，拾得手持一荷，谐音取意为"和合"。和合二仙是婚姻之神。旧时，有钱人家办喜事，要在新人拜天地的正堂中间挂一幅"和合二仙"的中堂。

Originally the god of harmony was Wan Hui of the Tang Dynasty but was replaced by Han Shan and Shi De during the transition of the Ming and Qing dynasties. Han Shan with a box in his hand and Shi De with a lotus flower combine to mean harmony on account of the same pronunciation. The two gods of harmony are guardians of marriage. In old customs, households of decent fortune would hang up a portrait of the two in the central hall where the newlyweds bow to heaven and earth for gratitude and blessings.

◎中华五福吉祥图典

喜

福 禄 寿 喜 财

和合二圣

The two gods of harmony

清雍正十一年，封天台寒山大士为"和圣"，拾得大士为"合圣"，遂将两人变成和合之神。中国讲和为贵，和合二圣给人带来和合，人们希望和合如意，和合美满，永远和合。图中以二圣手中的荷、如意以及美人蕉等寓意。

In the 11th year of the reign of Yongzheng of the Qing Dynasty, the title of "saint harmony" was conferred upon Han Shan and "saint peace" upon Shi De, making them both the gods of harmony and peace. China values harmony and desires eternal peace and stability and on this account, the two gods are highly cherished and respected. In the picture, the lotus flower, *ruyi*, and canna plant combine to convey the wish for peace, harmony, and smoothness in all things.

中华五福吉祥图典

喜 福 禄 寿 喜 财

和合如意

Harmony and heart-content

　　图以和合二仙手中的圣物"盒"
与"荷"表示"和合"。中国人视灵
芝为神物，传说食之不仅可使人生翼
乘云，轻身避水，长生不死，还能令
亡者起死回生。如意头取灵芝形取其
吉祥，"和合如意"寓意和睦相处、
称心如意。

The box and the lotus flower stand for harmony and peace. The Chinese people see the glossy
ganoderma as an object of miracle – it is believed
that after eating glossy ganoderma, people become
so light that they can walk on clouds and fly over
water, have eternal life and return to life from
death. The head of the *ruyi* is shaped like a
glossy ganoderma for the message it conveys – harmony and heart-content.

中华五福吉祥图典

喜

福禄寿喜财

喜
Happiness

和和美美

Harmony and happiness

夏荷、冬梅均为吉祥花卉。以
"荷"谐音"和",朵朵荷花示"和和"。
以"梅"谐音"美",朵朵梅花示"美
美"。旧时讲究"和为贵",在外做事
讲究和气生财,在家生活讲究和和睦
睦。"和和美美"多表示对新婚夫妇的
祝福,夫妻和美,白头偕老。

Lotus flowers, standing for harmony, and
plum blossoms, standing for happiness, both con-
nect with good fortune. As concord is treasured
both for family life and businesses, people tend to
pay a lof of attention to this value. To be harmonious and happy is a wish for newlyweds.

中华五福吉祥图典

喜

福 禄 寿 喜 财

喜
Happiness

金衣百子

High rank and 100 children

杜甫诗："两个黄鹂鸣翠柳，一行白鹭上青天。"韦应物诗："独怜幽草涧边生，上有黄鹂深树鸣。"黄鹂常被写入诗中，其雄鸟羽毛金黄，如身披金衣。以黄鹂的金羽，寓身披金袍，官居高位。以石榴多子，寓百子绕膝，富贵绵长。

Yellowbirds are often mentioned by poets in their works as an expression of love for Mother Nature. Male yellowbirds wear golden feathers which imply officials wearing golden gown and the pomegranates mean many children, lasting fortune and riches.

◎中华五福吉祥图典

喜

福 禄 寿 喜 财

宜 子 孙

Beneficial to one's children

　　萱草作为吉祥物，是因其有忘忧、宜男的特性。古代常以萱代母，萱草常植于北堂之畔，北堂为周礼规定的母亲之居所，以萱堂示母居，母亲康健，有宜子孙。《本草经》："萱一名忘忧。"《草木记》："妇女怀孕，佩其花则生男。"

Day lilies are grass of good fortune and are believed to be able to relieve worries and good to get male offsprings. In the past, day lilies were often used as alternative names for mothers and planted next to the north hall where mothers resided in accordance with the rituals of the Zhou Dynasty. It's said that by wearing day lilies, a pregnant woman would give birth to a boy.

171

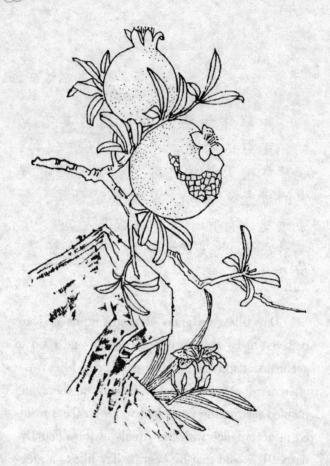

宜男多子

*Suitable to male offspring
and many children*

唐·李峤《萱》："屐步寻芳草，
忘忧自结丛。黄英开养性，绿叶正依
笼。色湛仙人露，香传少女风，还依
北堂下，曹植动雄文。"魏·曹植《宜
男花颂》："草号宜男，既晔且贞。"
作为吉祥物，以萱示"宜男"，以石
榴示"多子"。

Day lilies as grass of good fortune are substi-
tute names for mothers. Beautiful poems have been
composed to sing tribute to their beauty and great
qualities such as benefiting one's children, and
brilliance and virtuousness at the same time. Day
lilies are particularly good to get male offspring
while pomegranates indicate a great number of
children.

◎中华五福吉祥图典

喜 福 禄 寿 喜 财

弥勒送子

Maitreya sends over children

弥勒佛是佛教中三世佛中的未来
佛，由于其笑容可鞠深受人们欢迎，
还赋予他送子功能，有了"五子闹弥
勒"之图。家中供奉此图，可得子。
佛本无性，在中国却赋予了男女。在
佛教中，送子女神是观音，送子男神
是弥勒佛。

Of the three representations of past, present
and future, Maitreya was the future god and the
most popular. People really liked him because of
his amiable smile and believed he had the power
of sending people children. Families that wished
for children would hang up the picture of
"Maitreya at play with five kids" and their wish
would become true. While Buddha is gender-neu-
tral, the Chinese have worshipped Goddess of
Mercy as the child sending goddess and Maitreya
as the child sending god.

春燕剪柳

*Spring swallows cut
out willow leaves*

《诗经》："燕燕于飞，差池其羽。"燕，古称玄鸟，又名天女，还有"吉祥鸟"之称。燕是春天的象征，与春光同来，故又有"春燕"之称。燕喜双飞双栖，婚联中常以燕来祝吉。"双飞燕侣燕双飞。""春燕剪柳"寓新婚夫妇美满和谐。

Swallows, called birds of love, are mentioned in literature at a very early time. They come with spring and are hence also known as spring swallows. Swallows have the habit of flying and perching in pairs so their images often appear on marriage couplets for congratulations of luck. "Spring swallows cut out willow leaves" implies happy and harmonious couples.

中华五福吉祥图典

喜

福 禄 寿 喜 财

喜
Happiness

積善之家，必有餘慶

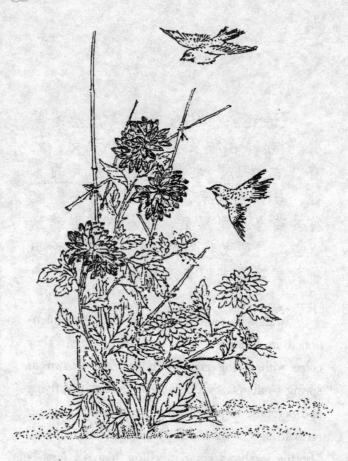

举家欢乐

Happy family life

《周易·坤》："积善之家，必有余庆；积不善之家，必有余殃。"《汉书·东平思王刘宇传》："福善之门莫美于和睦，患咎之首莫大于内离。""菊花"与"举家"谐音，黄雀的"黄"与"欢"谐音，合为"举家欢乐"，寓意家庭幸福。

Old Chinese literature comments that families which emphasize concord and unity are sure to have good fortune while those that fail to do so shall definitely encounter disasters. It also teaches people that households of happiness and good luck are harmonious whereas internal strife within a family is the worst enemy. Chrysanthemums sound like "the whole family", and yellowbirds sound like "happiness"; the two combine to mean happy family life.

中华五福吉祥图典

喜

福 禄 寿 喜 财

保子平安

Guardian over the safety of children

古代由于医学不发达，幼儿的成活率很低，人们就把保子平安的希望寄托于神明。七星娘娘作为护子之神，很受人们的崇拜。七星娘娘又叫七星夫人、七星妈、七娘夫人，画像为七位端庄的妇女，传说七星娘娘本是七仙女。

In ancient times, due to limited medical technology, infant mortality rate was high and the hope for the safety of babies rested with the gods. As the guardian of children, Goddess Seven Star was worshipped. Legend had it that Goddess Seven Star was actually the seven fairy girls. Drawn in the picture are seven women with dignified looks.

◎中华五福吉祥图典

喜

福 禄 寿 喜 财

保生平安

Life guardian

182

　　保生大帝是宋代民间医生吴本的
封号。吴本医术高明，慈悲济世，救
死扶伤，曾为宋仁宗皇后治好乳疾。
吴本死后，乡民为他修祠，后宋高宗
又为他建庙慈济宫，明末台湾也建了
慈济宫，吴本已成为保佑众生的保生
之神了。

　　Life Guardian is the title given to a folk doc-
tor Wu Ben of the Song Dynasty. Wu Ben had ad-
vanced medical skills and had a compassionate
heart. He cured many people, including the empress of Emperor Ren of the Song Dynasty. Wu's
country men built him a temple after his death.
Later, a Compassionate Temple was built in his
memory by Song Gao Zong, succeeded by another
temple of the same name in Taiwan in the late
Ming Dynasty. Wu has become the Life Guardian
of all human life.

中华五福吉祥图典

喜

福　禄　寿　喜　财

喜
Happiness

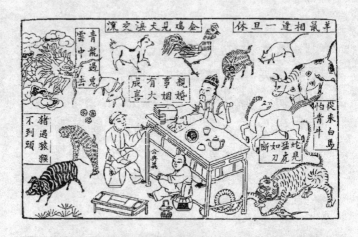

亲事有成

Harmonious marriages

Designs of Chinese Blessings

旧时的婚姻大事，是很迷信男女双方属性的相生、相克的。如：羊鼠相逢一旦休，从来白马怕青牛，蛇见猛虎如刀断，金鸡见犬泪交流，青龙过兔云中去，猪遇猿猴不到头等。过去不仅有属相图，还有专营亲事的算命先生。

In old customs, marriages were issues of great importance. People paid great attention to what years the boy and the girl were born in and what their symbolic animals were. Some symbolic animals were said to be incompatible with each other. If people with these symbolic animals married their marriage would not be happy. For example, goat and rat, horse and ox, snake and tiger, rooster and dog, dragon and rabbit, boar and monkey, etc. In the past, there were not only charts of the zodiac but also soothsayers that were engaged in marriage telling.

彎
彎
順

弯弯顺

Good fortune after many

twists and turns

诸事顺利，是人们的希望。但
"顺"的取得，往往要经过曲折，努
力过弯才能取顺。俗语："大丈夫能
屈，能伸。""小不忍，则乱大谋。"
"大难之后必有后福。"唐诗："山重
水复疑无路，柳暗花明又一村。""弯
弯顺"祝人好运。

It is the hope of everyone to be smooth in all
things. But, more often than not things get done
only after twists and turns. Idioms say that a man
of lofty goals can bear pressure and bad treatment.
Intolerance of minor insults will ruin great pro-
jects, and that only those who have suffered will
enjoy a great life. The picture here tells people
that things do not come easy and good luck comes
at the end.

中华五福吉祥图典

喜

福 禄 寿 喜 财

室上大吉

*Great fortune to the
whole family*

鸡为吉祥之神禽。《春秋运斗枢》: "立衡星散为鸡。"《韩诗外传》称鸡有文武勇仁信五德。《风俗通》云除夕 "以雄鸡着门上, 以和阴阳。" 室即家, 图中以 "石" 谐音 "室" 以 "大公鸡" 谐音 "大吉"。"室上大吉" 为阖家大吉大利。

Chicken are divine birds of good luck. In literature they are said to be gentle, valiant, brave, kind, and faithful. Customs have it that roosters on gates on Chinese New Year's eve bring peace to the household. In the picture, the stone stands for family, and the rooster stands on it for great luck. Therefore the message is great fortune to the whole family.

中华五福吉祥图典

喜

福 禄 寿 喜 财

姻缘圆满

Harmonious marriage fate

中华五福吉祥图典

　　明清时期，民间就有新郎、新娘在洞房同拜床神的习俗。有诗云："买糖迎灶帝，酌酒祀床公。"祭祀床神由来已久，此风俗在宋朝就已流行。床神有公、婆二位，传说周文王夫妇生有百子，多子多福，被尊为床公、床母。

In the Ming and Qing dynasties, it was customary for the bride and groom to offer sacrifice to the gods of bed in their new bedroom. The offerings could be candy and wine. Such practice actually became popular as early as in the Song Dynasty. There were two gods of bed, one male, one female. Legend has it that King Wen of Zhou and his empress had up to 100 children and are called the god and goddess of bed.

喜

福 禄 寿 喜 财

喜
Happiness

姻缘美满

Harmonious marriage fate

《清嘉录》载：因床母贪杯，床公好茶，故以酒祀床母，以茶祀床公，此为"男茶女酒"。旧时还有"安床"之俗，结婚的头几天要在洞房安放新床。安放新床要按男女生辰八字选位，择良辰吉日安床，安床当晚要拜床公床母。

Records have it that the goddess of bed likes wine and the god of bed likes tea, so these two are placed on marriage beds for blessings. According to ancient customs, the marriage bed should be placed in the new bedroom a few days ahead of wedding. The position of the bed and the date to place the bed should be in compliance with the hours of birth of the two newlyweds. Sacrifices should be offered to the god and goddess of bed on the same day.

◎中华五福吉祥图典

喜

福 禄 寿 喜 财

皆大欢喜

All is well and ends well

北京潭柘寺弥勒殿有联："大肚能容，容天下难容之事；开口便笑，笑世间可笑之人。"弥勒佛是中国人最喜欢的佛，他大度，他能消灾去病，保佑平安。旧时多子多福，有"五男二女"之说，供奉五子弥勒，即可多得贵子。

A couplet in the Maitreya Hall of Tanzhe Temple of Beijing reads like this: "His big stomach serves to accommodate all things of the world hard for man to bear; his large smile shows his good-humored disapproval of the detestable". Maitreya was the most popular Buddha for the Chinese thanks to his generosity and his power of healing and protection. Seven children – five boys and two girls, were the desirable number for traditional Chinese families and to achieve this end, a statue or picture of Maitreya with five kids was worshipped.

中华五福吉祥图典

喜

福禄寿喜财

安平保永　引指人貴

贵人指引

*Guidance of some wise
helpful men*

旧时过春节时，道士常以木刻印刷的符箓赠给春游寺观或进香祈福的人，名曰"旺相"，祝施主岁首新春福寿康宁，借此得到布施。"旺相"符箓有多种，此图上有"贵人指引"、"银马民符"，下有"大成北斗上元星君百解符咒。"

In the past, during the Chinese New Year, Taoist priests would give away wooden printed signs to tourists or worshippers to wish the donators good fortune, health, and peace in the new year in exchange of the donations they get. There are many kinds of signs like these and printed on this one at present are words that say "the guidance of some wise and helpful men", "riches to one's delight", and "a heavenly god blesses the donator and saves him from all difficulties".

中华五福吉祥图典

喜 福 禄 寿 喜 财

送子张仙

Zhang Xian sends
over children

图文："此仙本姓张，流落在下方；箭射云中犬，子孙不受伤。"说张仙乃五代后蜀皇帝孟昶，后蜀被宋太祖灭，花蕊夫人送到宋朝皇宫。她常怀念其夫，故画孟昶射猎图挂于卧室，太祖问之，花蕊诡称乃蜀中送子张仙。

The caption on the picture describes who Zhang Xian is – a fairy who fell to lead the life of a human; he shoots dogs in the clouds to keep the children from getting hurt. Legend has it that Zhang Xian was actually the emperor of a Sichuan state put out by the first emperor of the Song Dynasty. His wife, later sent to the Song palace, hung up her husband's portrait showing him hunting in her bedroom to release her pain of yearning. When questioned by the Song Emperor, she lied that he was Zhang Xian, the Sichuan god who sent children to those without.

哈哈二仙

The two gods of harmony

Designs of Chinese Blessings

《两湖游览志》："宋时杭城以腊月祀万回哥哥，其像蓬头笑面，祀之可使人在万里之外，亦能回家，故曰万回。"此种传说源于唐·段成式的《酉阳杂俎》：和合本是一人。和合二仙也称哈哈二仙，是团圆神、喜庆神。

Travelogue records that in Hongzhou during the Song Dynasty, memorial ceremonies were held for brother Wan Hui during the last month of the lunar calendar. It was believed that by offering sacrifices to Wan Hui (meaning return from 10,000miles away), who worn a smiling face with disheveled hair, beloved ones could return home no matter how far away they were. Legends from the Tang Dynasty tell people that the two gods of harmony are actually one. Known as the two gods of *haha* as well, gods of harmony are gods of re-union and celebrations.

201

喜
Happiness

鸳鸯合气

*Harmony between husband
and wife*

晋·崔豹《古今注》："鸳鸯，水鸟，凫类。雌雄未曾相离，人得其一，则一者相思死，故谓之匹鸟。"鸳鸯形影不离，雄左雌右。飞则共振翅，游则同戏水，栖则连翼，眠则交颈。如若丧偶，终身不匹。颇与"五伦"中的夫妻之义恰合。

As early as the Jin Dynasty, mandarin ducks were described as birds of loyalty and deep love. Mandarin ducks are never separated from each other. They fly together, swim together, touch each other in the wings when perching, and have their necks crossed when sleeping. If a partner dies, the other will stay single the rest of his life. This devotion serves as a perfect illustration of what husband and wife should be like according to traditional Chinese values.

◎中华五福吉祥图典

喜

福 禄 寿 喜 财

鸳鸯贵子

Loving couples and their darling children

婚联："缕结同心日丽屏间孔雀，莲开并蒂影摇池上鸳鸯。"鸳鸯是爱情忠贞，婚姻美满，夫妻和谐的象征。"五伦图"中以鸳鸯喻夫妻。"鸳鸯贵子"寓夫妻恩爱，连生贵子。在旧礼仪中桂子、桂花及莲子等常被寄予"贵子"之寓义。

A wedding couplet compares a happy couple to a pair of mandarin ducks and two lotus flowers that grow on one stem. Mandarin ducks serve as the symbol of devoted love, happy marriage, and harmonious married life. They refer to husband and wife in the five cardinal relationships of feudal China. In Chinese folk custom, lotus seeds and sweet-scented osmanthus are often borrowed to mean "valuable son". So the picture here implies conjugal love and bearing child after child.

◎中华五福吉祥图典

喜

福禄寿喜财

鸾凤和鸣

Pleasant marriage life

《山海经》: "西南三百里曰女床之山⋯⋯有鸟焉，其状如翟而五采文，名曰鸾鸟，见则天下安宁。"鸾是传说中凤凰一类的鸟。后人常以"鸾凤"喻夫妻，以"鸾凤和鸣"喻夫妻和谐。《梧桐雨》: "夜同寝，昼同行，恰似鸾凤和鸣。"

Ancient Chinese records have description of the bird *luan*, a phoenix-like bird. It has colorful feathers and its appearance brings peace to the world. A legendary foul like the phoenix, *luan* is often mentioned in conjunction with the phoenix to refer to spouses. A phoenix and a *luan* singing together refers to a marriage and a life of great concord. As another poem has it, (devoted husband and wife) would act together during the day and sleep together at night just like the phoenix and *luan* do.

中华五福吉祥图典

喜 福 禄 寿 喜 财

彩凤祥云

Colorful phoenixes and

lucky clouds

Designs of Chinese Blessings

《宋书·符瑞志》谓凤凰："蛇头燕颔，龟背鳖腹，鹤顶鸡喙，鸿前鱼尾，青首骈翼，鹭立而鸳鸯思。"凤凰是集众鸟之美的瑞鸟。《旧唐书·郑肃传》："天瑞有五色云，人瑞有郑仁丧。"祥云为祥瑞之云，"彩凤祥云"示吉祥。

Historical records from the Song Dynasty give such an account of a phoenix: it has the head of a snake, the chin of a swallow, the back of a turtle, the belly of a soft-shelled turtle, the crown of a crane, the beak of a chicken, the front of a swan, the tail of a fish, blue in the face with two wings, stands like a heron and are in pairs like the mandarin ducks. Phoenixes are lucky birds that combine the beauty of all birds. Colorful clouds are believed to be an indication of good fortune. Put together, colorful phoenixes and lucky clouds imply happiness and good fortune.

◎中华五福吉祥图典

喜

福禄寿喜财

喜
Happiness

喜 上 加 喜

Happiness upon happiness

　　《诗经·邶风·谷风》："宴尔新婚，如兄如弟。"《诗经·小雅·常棣》："妻子好合，如鼓瑟琴。"人逢喜事精神爽，新婚之时自是乐在心头，喜上眉梢。《花镜》："琼玑立骨，物外佳人，群芳领袖。"梅花常被比作美人。

Ancient Chinese literature described newlyweds as brothers of the same parents and as smooth music played on string instruments. As one is always refreshed and energetic when visited by happiness, people concerned are naturally joyful at heart and in appearance. Plum blossoms are flowers of unique character and grace and are hence often considered to incarnate beauty.

◎中华五福吉祥图典

喜

福 禄 寿 喜 财

喜上眉梢

Jubilance

喜联："金鸡踏桂题婚礼，喜鹊登梅报佳音。"春联："红梅吐蕊迎新春，喜鹊登枝唱丰年。"《天宝遗事·灵鹊报喜》："时人之家，闻鹊声，皆曰喜兆，故谓灵鹊报喜。"鹊是报喜之鸟，梅是报春之花，以喜上"梅"梢谐音，喜上"眉"梢。

A wedding couplet reads that "a rooster on sweet-scented osmanthus announces the good news of a wedding and magpies on plum trees tell of good tidings". A Chinese New Year couplet reads that "red plum flowers bloom to greet a new spring, magpies perch on a branch to foretell a good autumn harvest". In Chinese customs, magpies are birds of good luck and their twitter is a sign of good fortune. Magpies announce happiness, plum blossoms tell spring has come. As plum sounds like "eyebrow" in pronunciation, the picture means "happy look".

◎中华五福吉祥图典

喜

福禄寿喜财

喜从天降

*Happiness descends
from heaven*

《尔雅·释虫·注》："小蜘蛛长脚者，俗呼为喜子。"唐时人多画蜘蛛于墙上，称为"壁钱。"《毛诗草木鸟兽鱼虫疏》："此虫来著人衣，当有亲客至，有喜也。"《广五行记》："蜘珠集于军中及人家，有喜事。"蜘蛛现，喜事兆。

Ancient Chinese literature recorded that small spiders were called "seeds of happiness" in folk language. During the Tang Dynasty, spiders were drawn on the wall and called "wall money". Other records tell that where spiders gather in the army or at home, it is a sign that happy events are about to occur, seeing a spider is the sign that luck is on its way.

中华五福吉祥图典

喜

福 禄 寿 喜 财

喜
Happiness

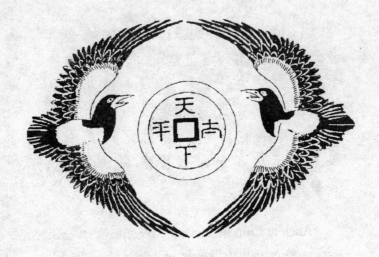

喜在眼前

Happiness right at

present

我国最早的货币是以贝壳充当的。至商周时，开始用青铜铸币。后来也有用金、银铸币的。历代铜钱上多铸有制作年号及祝福国运昌盛的吉语。铜钱形多为圆形中有方孔，"孔"也称"钱眼"，倒置喻"眼前"，与喜鹊组成喜在眼前。

The first currency in China consisted of shells. Coins minted with bronze started in the Shang and Zhou dynasties. Later, coins of gold and silver were used as well. Coins of copper were often minted with the year of production and wished the nation to be prosperous. Copper coins were round shaped with a square hole in the center called money hole. Inverted, money hole reads like "at present" in Chinese. Jointly with magpies, the picture means happiness right at present.

◎中华五福吉祥图典

喜

福 禄 寿 喜 财

喜
Happiness

喜在眼前

喜在眼前

Happiness right at present

据《宋书》记载，徐羡官拜司空时，有两只喜鹊在太极殿的飞檐上鸣叫。喜为"五福"之一，喜鹊为喜鸟又带喜，故在吉祥图中多喻喜。此图中一富人，眼前有两只喜鹊，看来又要有"徐羡官拜司空"的仕途之喜在眼前了。

Historical books record that when Xu Xian was given the title of minister of public works, two magpies were calling on the roof. Happiness is one of the five good fortunes, and, since magpies are birds of happiness and bear that character in their names, they often appear in pictures to indicate happiness. In the present picture a rich man is watching two magpies right in front of him. It seems a promotion is just about to occur again.

中华五福吉祥图典

喜

福 禄 寿 喜 财

喜
Happiness

喜報春光

喜报春光

Announcement of the

arrival of spring

宋·陈亮《梅花》诗："一朵忽先报，百花背后香，欲传春消息，不怕雪里藏。"梅开花在冬春之交，亦称报春花。喜报春光，迎来了一年最美好的季节。李世民《首春》："寒随穷律变，春逐鸟声开。初风飘带柳，晓雪间花梅。"

Chen Liang of the Song Dynasty wrote a poem about the plum flowers: "One plum flower leads the rest in fragrance and beauty; they rush to announce the arrival of spring though hidden in snow". In full bloom during the turn of winter and spring, plum flowers are also called harbingers-of-spring as they bloom with the coming of the best time of the year. Li Shimin, the first emperor of the Tang Dynasty composed a poem about spring: "The cold season has changed with a bird singing spring; willow trees wave in a soft breeze while plum flowers bloom amongst the snow".

中华五福吉祥图典　喜　福禄寿喜财

喜
Happiness

月下老人

喜结良缘

A happy marriage fate

有情来相会，姻缘一线牵。传说唐朝人韦固，见一老人靠着布口袋在月下翻书，便问老人看的什么书，老人说是天下婚书；又问口袋中有何物，老人说袋中都是红绳，此绳一系男女双方便定终身。月老一线牵，男女结良缘。

A legend tells the story of the matchmaker: he was seen leaning against a cloth bag reading a book under the moonlight. When asked what he was reading and what was in his bag, he answered he was reading marriage papers of all people on the earth and in the bag there were red strings that tied man and woman together for life. Once the red thread is tied by the matchmaker, the man and woman concerned get united in marriage.

◎中华五福吉祥图典

喜

福禄寿喜财

喜鹊登梅

Magpies on plum trees

《易卦》："鹊者阳鸟，先物而动，先事而应。"有感应予兆的神奇本领。《西京杂记》："乾鹊噪而行人至，蜘蛛集而百事喜。"鹊噪也予示客人的到来。《风俗通》："织女七夕当渡河，使鹊为桥。"鹊集众喜于一身，登梅报佳音。

Ancient Chinese records described magpies as birds of prophecy: magically, they can tell things ahead of time. Other records say that magpies announce the arrival of guests just like spiders foretell happy events. Another function the magpies play according to ancient stories is that they serve as the bridge when the cowboy and the weaving girl meet over the Milky Way yearly on July the 7th. Happiness incarnate, magpies on plum trees are a typical symbol of forthcoming good events.

中华五福吉祥图典

喜 福 禄 寿 喜 财

新韶如意

All to the heart's content
at the new spring

梁·简文帝《答湘东王书》："暮春美景，风云韶丽。"宋·范成大《初夏》诗："晴丝千尺挽韶光，百舌无声燕子忙。"韶，意为美好。韶光、韶华，为美好时光。新韶，则喻新年或新春。"新韶如意"，表示新年伊始，万事如意。

The beauty of spring has been under the poetic description of many Chinese emperors and men of letters. Spring brings warmth, swallows, green trees, and colorful flowers. Success and everything to the heart's content is the wish of the beginning of every year at spring time.

福增贵子

*More good fortune
and children*

旧时，由于"男尊女卑"，妇女在家庭中的地位往往是由其是否生子所决定的。母以子为贵，祈盼多生贵子的吉祥图很多。桂音谐"贵"，桂花不仅是象征富贵的吉祥物，桂子、桂花还常被赋予"贵子"的寓意。桂花与蝙蝠合为"福增贵子"。

In ancient China, women's role in the family depended on whether she had borne male children. Due to such a traditional positioning, women looked forward to having children and pictures on the theme became popular. Sweet-scented osmanthus is the symbol of nobility and fortune and their seeds and flowers are often associated with "son". Sweet-scented osmanthus and bats together mean "more good fortune and sons".

中华五福吉祥图典

喜

福 禄 寿 喜 财

榴开百子

A cut-up pomegranate with numerous seeds

据《北史》载："北齐高延宗纳赵郡李祖收之女为妃，高延宗临幸李家时，岳母以两个大石榴相赠。帝不明其意，大臣魏收说：'石榴房中多子，王新婚，妃母欲子孙众多。'"旧时婚嫁，在新房放切开露子的石榴，盼多生贵子。

Historical records give a detailed account of an emperor receiving two large pomegranates from his mother-in-law when he visited her home. Seeing that the emperor was puzzled, his minister said that, as newlyweds, the mother-in-law wished him and her daughter would have a lot of children just like the fruit had a lot of seeds. In old customs, pomegranates cut open to show the seeds were placed in the bedroom of the newlyweds, implying they were expected to have a lot of children.

Happiness

榴开百子

A cut-up pomegranate with numerous seeds

古人称石榴"千房同膜，千子如一"。石榴作为吉祥物是多子的象征。早在六朝石榴就被作为生子、多子的祝颂吉物。在中国的传统器物上，多有石榴的图案。在吉祥图中，"榴开百子"多以门童的形式出现，此图与下图是一对门童。

Ancient people said pomegranates have 1000 rooms with the same membrane and 1000 seeds of the same look. The fruit has long been regarded as the symbol of fertility. The earliest records of its use as objects of eulogy and congratulations may be traced back to the Six Dynasties. Designs of pomegranates can be seen on traditional Chinese utensils. As a picture of good luck, "pomegranates with many seeds" often appear on doors and this picture forms a pair with the one following.

◎中华五福吉祥图典

喜

福禄寿喜财

榴开百子

A cut-up pomegranate with numerous seeds

《安石榴赋》："若榴者，天下之奇树，五州之名果也。是以属文之士或叙而赋之。遥而望之，焕若隋珠耀重渊；详而察之，灼若列宿出云间。千房同膜，千子如一，御饥疗渴，解醒止醉。"榴"千子如一"故与"多子"结缘。

An essay to pomegranates reads like this: "Marvelous trees are the pomegranates that bear wonderful fruits and win the praise of many literators. Gazed at from the distance, they shine like pearls; observed carefully, their brilliant seeds look like constellations from the skies. They have 1000 rooms with the same membrane and 1000 seeds of the same look. They serve to quench thirst and hunger and help people sober up from wine." Pomegranates stand for many children due to their abundant seeds.

喜
Happiness

榴开百子

A cut-up pomegranate with numerous seeds

旧时新婚，摆上枣和栗子，以示
"早生贵子"；摆上切开露子的石榴，
以示"多生贵子"，摆上花生，以示
"花着生"等。旧时婚联，也多有
"榴开百子"的内容，如："合欢花灿
双辉烛，竞艳榴开百子图。"祝有
"多子"之福。

In the old tradition, dates and chestnuts im-
plied "to have children at an early date",
pomegranates cut apart indicate "to have a lot of
children", and peanuts stand for "to have boys
and girls in turns". In wedding couplets of old
times, pomegranates were also mentioned and were
associated with "many children".

鹤庆吉祥

Happiness and good fortune

《花镜》："鹤，一名仙鸟，羽族之长也。"鹤为长寿吉祥之鸟。磬为"五瑞"之一，也位列"八宝"，磬本为吉祥之物，又与"庆"谐音。"鹤庆"又有"贺庆"之音。旧时磬常作喜庆礼仪的装饰，击磬之声，祥云之状，合为"鹤庆吉祥"。

Cranes were considered fairy birds and the head of the birds' family in ancient records. Cranes represented longevity and good fortune. Chime stone, one of the five objects of good fortune and among the eight treasures, coincides with the word "celebration" in reading in Chinese. In ancient times, chime stones were often used as decorations for rituals of celebrations. The sound of the stone chiming and the sight of lucky clouds combine to mean happiness and good fortune.

喜
Happiness

聪明伶俐

Bright and smart children

聪：听觉灵敏；明：视觉敏锐。
伶俐：灵活，乖巧，干脆，爽利。聪
明伶俐多用于对聪慧儿童的称赞。
"葱"与"聪"谐音。藕心空明透亮，
示"明"。"菱"谐音"伶"，"荔"谐
音"俐"，合为"聪明伶俐。"寓意多
生聪明伶俐的贵子。

Acute hearing, bright eyesight, and flexibility and alacrity in doing things are words of praises for smart children. "Spring onion" sounds the same as "acute hearing"; "lotus root" stands for "bright" as there are holes in the center. Water chestnut and litchi sound the same as "cleverness". The picture implies an expectation for brighter children.

麟趾呈祥

May the children be
wise and capable

《诗经》："麟之趾，振振公子，于嗟麟兮。"是说周文王的子孙知礼行善，后多用于赞颂子孙之贤慧。麟趾呈祥在旧时多作为婚典喜联的横披，以祝生育仁厚之后代。在祝贺生子的联中也有："石麟果是真麟趾，雏凤清于老凤声。

The *Book of Songs* of ancient China mentioned the toes of the unicorns to praise the children of King Wen of Zhou as they observed rituals and did good deeds. Later, the toes of the unicorns turned to be words of praise for the wisdom and capabilities of children. The phrase "happiness and good fortune with unicorns toes" is often used as a horizontal hanging scroll for wedding celebrations to wish for the benevolence of the newlyweds' offsprings. Couplets for congratulations on childbirth may also refer to unicorns toes.

喜
Happiness

麟凤呈祥

A peaceful and stable society

麒麟为仁兽，蹄不踏青草和昆虫，不群居，不旅行，不饮污池。凤凰是神禽，不啄活虫，不折生草，不群居，不乱翔，非梧桐不栖，非竹实不食。《吴越春秋》："禹养万民，凤凰栖于树，麒麟步于庭。""麟凤呈祥"寓天下太平。

Unicorns are kind beasts that do not step on grass and insects, stay by themselves at a definite place, and never drink from waste water. Phoenixes are divine fowls that do not peck on live insects or grass, stay by themselves, fly for a definite purpose, and perch only on Chinese parasol trees. The picture implies a peaceful and stable society.

图书在版编目（CIP）数据

中华五福吉祥图典．喜／黄全信主编；李迎春译．—北京：华语教学
出版社，2003.1
ISBN 7-80052-892-8
I.中… Ⅱ.①黄… ②李… Ⅲ. 图案 - 中国 - 图集 Ⅳ. J522
中国版本图书馆 CIP 数据核字（2002）第 097609 号

选题策划：单　瑛　英文翻译：李迎春
责任编辑：蔡希勤　封面设计：唐少文
英文编辑：韩　晖　印刷监制：佟汉冬

中华五福吉祥图典——喜

主编　黄全信

*

©华语教学出版社
华语教学出版社出版
（中国北京百万庄路 24 号）
邮政编码 100037
电话：010-68995871 / 68326333
传真：010-68326333
电子信箱: hyjx @263.net
北京通州次渠印刷厂印刷
中国国际图书贸易总公司海外发行
（中国北京车公庄西路 35 号）
北京邮政信箱第 399 号　邮政编码 100044
新华书店国内发行
2003 年（32 开）第一版
（汉英）
ISBN 7-80052-892 -8 / H · 1428（外）
9—CE—3529P
定价：26.00 元